# The Reference Interview Today

# The Reference Interview Today

*Negotiating and Answering Questions*
*Face to Face, on the Phone, and Virtually*

Dave Harmeyer

ROWMAN & LITTLEFIELD
Lanham • Boulder • New York • Toronto • Plymouth, UK

Published by Rowman & Littlefield
4501 Forbes Boulevard, Suite 200, Lanham, Maryland 20706
www.rowman.com

10 Thornbury Road, Plymouth PL6 7PP, United Kingdom

British Library Cataloguing in Publication Information Available

**Library of Congress Cataloging-in-Publication Data**

Harmeyer, Dave, 1956–
The reference interview today : negotiating and answering questions face to face, on the phone, and virtually / Dave Harmeyer.
pages cm
Includes bibliographical references and index.
ISBN 978-0-8108-8815-9 (pbk. : alk. paper) – ISBN 978-0-8108-8816-6 (ebook)
Reference services (Libraries) 2. Electronic reference services (Libraries) I. Title.
Z711.H419 2014
025.5'2–dc23
2013037114

∞™ The paper used in this publication meets the minimum requirements of American National Standard for Information Sciences Permanence of Paper for Printed Library Materials, ANSI/NISO Z39.48-1992.

Printed in the United States of America

Sheli
*Wife, mother, encourager, friend*

Breanna Grace
*1st miracle daughter*

Sophia Janelle
*2nd miracle daughter*

# Contents

# Foreword

In the early 1990s, I became acquainted with Dave Harmeyer. At the time, he was a graduate student in the Graduate School of Library and Information Science (now the Department of Information Studies). During the course of his graduate studies, he wrote what I considered a publishable paper entitled "Potential Collection Development Bias: Some Evidence on a Controversial Topic in California." We worked closely together on it until his graduation, at the end of the fall term 1993.

You can imagine my pleasure when he learned that *College and Research Libraries* would publish his manuscript in March of 1995 (56:101–11). Placing a great deal of confidence in his scholarship, I asked him to serve as a guest lecturer in my DIS 245: "Information Access" classes (fall 2006). About the same time, he asked me to write a letter of recommendation for him when he applied to Pepperdine University's School of Education and Psychology; next, he asked me to serve on his EdD dissertation committee, and I did so willingly.

Given my reading of his dissertation, I believe that Dave has undertaken original work that sheds significant light on the nature of virtual/digital reference transactions. He has analyzed hundreds of reference transcriptions, which at the moment is a nearly unique achievement. As you may know, much of the scholarly history of reference transaction research has focused on the presumed difficulty of test questions, whereas Dave has actually looked at hundreds of real questions. His sociolinguistic analysis of these interviews should be quite enlightening for the profession.

Of course, he has been blogging as well (see *The Reference Interview Today*), and you will see that influence in the following pages. I love the idea of anything that will improve the quality of service rendered in our libraries, whether we are talking about checklists, flowcharts, or other systems analysis techniques. The point is that Dave has thirteen wonderful scenarios full of anecdotes, intuition, and evidence-based practices to help us out.

In short, as you read the collected chapters, I hope that you will agree that Dave Harmeyer's *The Reference Interview Today* will make an important contribution to our field, specifically in our shared interest of improving reference librarianship.

Dr. John V. Richardson Jr.<br>
UCLA Professor Emeritus of Information Studies<br>
September 2013

# Preface

The blog that augments this book at http://referenceinterview.word press.com/ has a tagline that describes the common ground in both blog and book: "Best Practices for the Reference Interview." So I was curious: What kind of competition is a best-practices book up against these days? According to the world's largest online public catalog, WorldCat, 13,044 books have the phrase *best practices* in their titles or tables of contents. [1] If you add the truncated term *librar** as a subject heading, that whittles it down to 134 books. And if you replace *librar** with *reference* as a subject heading, we now have 24 books published between 1993 and 2013. So, what compelling reasons make this book worth your time reading: things that those others have not already covered? Well, that depends on who you are . . .

## LIBRARY SCHOOL STUDENTS AND THEIR FACULTY

If you are, as I was, a student in a credentialed or American Library Association–accredited master's program in library and information science, this book is for you. I have heard—and you may say it yourself someday—"No one ever effectively explained to me how to really conduct a successful reference interview." The thirteen scenarios here, set in both a public and an academic library, recall mostly real-life reference interview conversations informed by passionate intuition and, in some cases, evidence-based practices, as explained in chapter 16, "A Conceptual Model for Online Chat Reference Answer Accuracy." Each scenario is more than merely anecdotal. Imbedded in the stories are timeless principles. You may ask, "Are there really enduring principles for the reference interview that change little over time?" Well, one example to consider is Ranganathan's 1931 five laws of library science. [2] Most of Ranganathan's philosophical foundations of the modern library profession are imbedded in several of the reference interviews. There are thought-provoking questions at the end of each narrative, written within Bloom's taxonomy of learning domains, which encourage you to begin with factual-type questions before leading you toward progressively higher levels of learning, such as analyzing and evaluating. Finally, each of the thirteen situations has a place in the blog for you to continue the discussion with others on the topic of best practices for the reference interview today.

## THOSE WHO DO ANY LEVEL OF PUBLIC, ACADEMIC, SPECIAL, OR SCHOOL LIBRARY REFERENCE: NOVICE–EXPERT

I admit that it is not an easy task to suggest that you read this book. In addition to many well-written and useful field guides on the reference interview by specialists with decades of experience, you probably think that you do not need yet another primer on one of our most essential and sustainable professional tasks in the profession. All I can say is, you will miss out! You will miss out on a group of crazy, truthful stories written in the genre of British veterinary surgeon James Herriot's *All Creatures Great and Small*.[3] You will miss out on what the reference interview might look like in the year 2025. You will miss out on what *Harry Potter and the Secrets of Hogwarts* has to do with the reference interview. Finally, you will miss out on contributing toward improving the reference interview for the next generation of reference professionals built on a common narrative as found in the book and continued in the blog *The Reference Interview Today*.

## EVERYONE ELSE

This is just my bias . . . I think the thirteen stories stand on their own as entertaining ways to crack the door just a little on what it really is like to work as a professional reference librarian. They kill the stereotype of what a librarian does at the reference desk, on the phone, in chat, and in places such as Second Life and even the future. Those who read these scenarios will be stronger advocates for the profession and its changing, challenging, risky future. And in addition to inspiring future library and information professionals . . . who knows . . . if the right community learns about this work, these thirteen unassuming stories about a passionately committed reference professional at the beginning of the twenty-first century might grow into something akin to the television episodes of the endearing, rural, midtwentieth-century veterinarian James Herriot.

# NOTES

1. Online Computer Library Center, WorldCat, accessed August 30, 2013.
2. Shiyali R. Ranganathan, *The Five Laws of Library Science* (London: Goldston, 1931).
3. James Herriot, *All Creatures Great and Small* (New York: St. Martin's Press, 1972).

# Acknowledgments

Janice Baskin
Director of Library Publications
Azusa Pacific University

Paul Gray
Dean of University Libraries
Azusa Pacific University

Farzin Madjidi
Professor, Graduate School of Education and Psychology
Pepperdine University

William Miller
Dean of University Libraries
Florida Atlantic University

Rita Pellen
Associate Dean of University Libraries
Florida Atlantic University

John V. Richardson
Professor Emeritus of Information Studies
University of California, Los Angeles

Jane Thorndike
Electronic Resources Coordinator
Azusa Pacific University

Margaret J. Weber
Dean of the Graduate School of Education and Psychology
Pepperdine University

*The Reference Librarian*

*Chapter One*

# Prologue

*Is the Reference Interview Dead?*

I was at my thirty-fifth high school reunion, and the inevitable question came up: "So, Dave, what do you do?" My answer, "I'm a librarian," drew back a response from someone whom I had not seen in decades along the lines of "Isn't everything available on the Internet? Why do we need libraries and librarians?" It did throw me off for a moment. I did not want to respond with "Well, I think you're wrong," then go on about the values that libraries and librarians provide that the Internet cannot. Before I share my answer, allow me to put a rather large parenthesis here and dare to ask the question, what *if* it were true?! What if library professionals are in some kind of blind denial? Libraries, librarians, reference, and particularly the reference interview are unnecessary because of technological advances. What other claims have been made that warrant us to seriously ask, is the reference interview dead?

For evidence, we need go no further than the field of library and information science itself. Dialogue within the ranks of the profession has squarely placed a question mark, ironically, on its own confidence in the practice of library reference. Although the following research studies, survey results, and opinions examine reference either in a philosophical sense or from a more tangible perspective of the reference desk, each would have some effect on the sustainability of the subject of this book: the reference interview. It is unclear to me if the following nine librarians (their publications listed chronologically) are playing the role of an antagonist, a truthsayer, or both. What follow are brief summaries of what I think are their more persuasive reasons why reference, the reference desk, and consequently the reference interview are dead (or at least should be put out of their misery), and I will let you be the judge.

1

# EVIDENCE FOR THE DEATH OF REFERENCE AND THE REFERENCE INTERVIEW

William Miller's 1984 "What's Wrong with Reference? Coping with Success and Failure at the Reference Desk," in *American Libraries*.[1]

- Old, outdated reference books fill the shelves; new ones are not used.
- Librarians are uninformed about evolving technologies.
- Reference staff are fearful of change.
- Reference librarians are overcommitted, prone to burnout, and over-worked—real and imagined.
- Meager planners and managers.
- Perception that some are jealous of the younger, more active librarians.
- Perception that some younger, more active librarians think that others are a burden.
- Irritated, frustrated, bitter reference personnel.
- Adding new services to an already too full agenda.
- Reluctant to professional development.
- Unobtrusive studies show the reference desk to be mediocre in service.
- Answer accuracy is only around 50 percent.
- Shortcomings ignored by administrative decision makers.
- Time for personal renewal (sabbaticals) uncommon.
- Lack of adequate funding to properly staff service points.
- Task-saving machines take more work than what is worth the benefit.
- Using nonprofessionals at the reference desk delivers lower quality of service.
- Not getting at end user's real question by not asking clarifying questions.
- End users are triaged to create adequate time for *real* reference transactions.
- Annual library budgets increase above the rate of inflation.
- Decision makers show little regard for reference personnel's professional growth or well-being.
- Monotonous tasks, shallow questions, and repetitive directional questions produce reference staff without smiles.

Jerry Campbell's 2000 "Clinging to Traditional Reference Services: An Open Invitation to Libref.Com," in *Reference and User Services Quarterly*.[2]

- For administrators, assessing reference is too multifaceted and unclear.
- Reference is growing less relevant to library users.
- The 55 percent problem—users get correct answers from librarians only 55 percent of the time.[3]

- Members of the Association of Research Libraries (120 of the largest academic libraries in North America) report a significant decline in reference transactions.
- Library users prefer e-mail reference over face-to-face and phone.[4]
- Only small clusters of students and faculty actually use the reference services.
- Students want to take the trouble of finding a librarian to get a correct answer only about half the time.
- Reference librarians deny that face-to-face interviews are no longer relevant.
- The expertise of reference librarians has largely been left out of the digital information revolution.
- Future reference services are being designed and implemented by nonlibrarians.
- For-profit universities are working from an unconventional library model—no library and, therefore, no reference services.
- Students and faculty are more inclined to use an online answering service or search engine than walk into a library.

Joseph Janes's 2003 "What Is Reference For?" in *Reference Services Review.*[5]

- Conventional reference being replaced by for-profit services.
- The ubiquitous availability of end user–friendly, free, web-based information sources happens without reference librarians as mediators.
- Some seem to want reference continued to merely employ personnel.
- Reference statistics are dropping severely.
- Reference staff are unfamiliar with the changing reference interview preferences of end users.
- The quick response rate of Internet search engines cause reference staff to have significantly fewer fact-type questions.

Catherine Robinson and Peter Reid's 2007 "Do Academic Enquiry Services Scare Students?" in *Reference Services Review.*[6]

- Library users feel intimidated by librarians and the size and complexity of the library.
- Users are annoyed by librarians who appear to be too busy to answer a question or users who do not want to waste the time of busy reference staff.

- One negative event with a librarian ("Turn off your cell phone") keeps that patron from approaching that librarian in the future.
- Users prefer to ask a friend, teaching assistant, or professor about their library needs rather than approach an unknown librarian.
- Users appear to be most anxious about library equipment when reference staff are explaining how to use it, especially when others or acquaintances are nearby.
- Patrons do not ask questions at the reference desk, because they do not want to be viewed as foolish.

Susan M. Ryan's 2008 "Reference Transactions Analysis: The Cost-Effectiveness of Staffing a Traditional Academic Reference Desk," in the *Journal of Academic Librarianship.*[7]

- In this study at a university with a student full-time equivalent of 2,500, 89 percent of reference desk queries could be answered by nonlibrarians.
- In this study, 36.3 percent of questions were found to be directional or machine oriented (how to run the microfilm machine) and did not need the expertise of a librarian.
- Pre-Internet searches using print indexes for, say, ten peer-reviewed articles took hours and required the help of a librarian, but in a digital environment, the same request takes thirty seconds without a librarian.
- Librarian-mediated help using subject headings is replaced by patrons searching with keywords ending in adequate results.
- Some reference desk professionals spend too much time at the desk doing nonreference work, such as explaining software use, changing toner cartridges, and troubleshooting network connections, in addition to the usual directional questions.
- In this study, librarians answered research-type questions fewer than four times daily.
- One large university (37,000 students) reported an 88 percent drop in reference desk questions between 1991 and 2004.[8]
- Reference desk librarians lack constant, reliable, measurable accountability for the questions they answer.[9]

Sara Tompson and Catherine Quinlan's 2011 "Reference Desk Renaissance: Connecting with Users in the Digital Age," in the *Association of College and Research Library's 2011 Conference Proceedings* (March 30–April 2, 2011).[10]

- Changes to a reference desk location have resulted in cloistered reference personnel hidden from intended users and physically distant from much of the print reference collection.
- From 1991 to 2004, the Association of Research Libraries reported a drop of 34 percent in reference transactions among its 124 members, averaging a 3.2 percent decline per year. [11]
- Some librarians had a perception that users could find information on their own with little difficulty and that the information would be valid and accurate.
- In-depth reference questions have ceased to be asked at the reference desk. [12]

Christy Stevens's 2013 "Reference Reviewed and Re-envisioned: Revamping Librarian and Desk-Centric Services with LibStARs and LibAnswers," in the *Journal of Academic Librarianship.* [13]

- The large decline in reference transactions from 1990 to 2010 is part of the overall declining usage of physical libraries.
- As early as 2003, authors documented that librarians were no longer getting as many quick, lookup questions because users were getting them from Google. [14]
- A librarian sitting at a desk doing other work causes patrons to hesitate before asking legitimate questions because of the perception that the librarian is too busy or even rude.
- Studies before 1983 found that end users perceived the reference desk as a place to ask only simple, quickly answered questions, not a place to go for longer research questions. [15]
- At the opening of the new University of California at Merced (September 2005), the library did not include a traditional reference desk but a student-staffed Library Services Desk and Helpdesk. [16]
- Reference staff are blinded, valuing the centrality of the reference desk far more than their end users. [17]

## HOPE FOR THE LIFE OF REFERENCE AND THE REFERENCE INTERVIEW

Before continuing with my answer to an old high school acquaintance at my thirty-fifth reunion, there is another side to the death of reference and the reference interview discussion. To provide a fairer, more equitable perspective of the aforementioned summaries, the same nine librarians also expressed suggestions toward establishing a more sustainable, thriving model of reference services. Again, in chronological order, the following are selected synopses of how these authors propose preventing reference and the reference interview from certain death.

William Miller (1984)[18]

- Provide more time to bond with library colleagues, more time to know relevant resources, and more time to be with the end user during the reference interview.
- As a reference department, attend overnight retreats to learn about library purpose and the profession and to refresh mental capacity.
- Continue to assess reference personnel in terms of good fit, their needed training, and number of exceptional years of work and to reassign when needed.
- Knowing that there are limitations to technology, use computers to increase efficiency, record and report statistics, and perform time-saving clerical tasks.
- Utilize paraprofessional and student staff at strategic locations with clear understandings that all but directional and rudimentary questions are to be referred to reference professionals.
- Experiment with cycling librarians off reference every few years so that they can experience professional tasks in other library departments and perhaps avoid burnout.
- Ask and provide answers to hard questions about traditional assumptions in regard to reference services.
- Do the hard work of strategic planning for the reference program.
- Faithfully perform a regular needs assessment for library users.

Jerry Campbell (2000)[19]

- Be an advocate for reference reform.
- Reconsider reference with an attitude of liberty and imagination.
- Get involved in Internet-based library and information reorganization.
- Advance the mission of reference without its current practices.
- Anticipate the next generation of information technology.
- Prepare to run reference where librarian and user are not together at the same time (asynchronous).
- Prepare to run the reference interview in real time where librarian and user are not together in the same place (distributed learning).

- Change your bad or neutral attitude toward web-based delivery of information and embrace it.
- Be prepared to give for-profit educational institutions compelling reasons why they should include a library and reference services in their business plan.
- Help build the next Ask Jeeves.

Joseph Janes (2003)[20]

- Continue to remember why reference was created initially: to meet the increasing diverse needs of patrons, caused by new, ever-increasing, complex information sources.
- Know assets and liabilities of emerging information technologies.
- Ask simple but deeper questions about next-generation reference services.
- Resist making new reference services mimic past forms.
- Attempt to predict relevant technology changes and use them to meet reference and reference interview goals.
- Tailor-make reference services, with its many choices, to match diversified library users' preferences, focusing on ways that they currently use information.
- Focus on natural strengths of reference and the reference interview to counteract end users' uninformed Internet searching attempts that result in too many or too few results that are irrelevant or even wrong.
- Understand the advantages of the reference interview over end users' self-attempts, such as discerning high-quality, valid, reliable, accurate, and timely information.

Catherine Robinson and Peter Reid (2007)[21]

- Create a consistent image that the job of the reference staff is question answering, done in a timely manner and in a way that sincerely makes the end user feel respected.
- Be ready to disarm the tendency of patrons to be shy, scared, or embarrassed—that they are asking too simple a question.
- When helping users with mechanical equipment (operating a microfilm machine, moving compact shelving), note that even the most self-assured patron can be anxious and uncomfortable with the device because of inexperience.
- Create inviting, friendly, and well-marked environments where reference transactions can take place.

- Exercise a wandering reference staff who proactively seek out patrons in need of help but resistant to leave computers or study areas.
- For online access to answers of reference questions, provide logical and clear approaches to timely and accurate answers that can be transacted in an anonymous way (synchronous and asynchronous).

Susan M. Ryan (2008)[22]

- Do not expect to learn reference transaction skills in graduate school but on the job using the print and online resources of a particular library.
- Implement on-call reference services—reference staff are not at the reference desk but available at a moment's notice.[23]
- Remove reference service at one or more locations and provide a one-stop service area staffed with professional and nonprofessional staff, meeting the multiple needs of circulation, general information, and short/long reference transactions.[24]
- Place reference transaction stations where student patrons hang out.[25]

Sara Tompson and Catherine Quinlan (2011)[26]

- Patrons in university and public settings need more, not less, help in accessing information in a digital environment that they might or might not successfully find on their own.[27]
- Authors who recommend that reference desks be closed also propose that librarians increase their role in instruction.
- In one poll of 350 English 101 students at Calvin College, 85 percent preferred reference help face-to-face versus e-mail, phone, or chat.[28]
- From 1995 to 2005, the Association of Research Libraries reported an average drop in reference questions of 47 percent, and 83 libraries reported a decline; however, 12 showed an increase.[29]
- In one university, specifically the University of Southern California, a 72 percent increase in reference queries in 2009 was attributed to a new library strategic plan that made public services more visible than any year before.
- Millennials (those born between 1980 and 2000) are inclined to use chat reference but also face-to-face reference with librarians who are friendly.[30]

Christy Stevens (2013)[31]

- Although there are fewer reference queries, those that are asked tend to require much more length in time, depth of view, and scholarly results than in the past.[32]
- Answers to reference questions are sometimes so complex that the librarian conducts more of a library instruction session (topic overview, search techniques, database demo, citation instruction) rather than a typical reference interview.[33]
- The growing percentage of complex research questions by student patrons would be more successfully answered in a scheduled, quiet office consultation.
- To increase the quality of reference, change the desk signage from Reference Desk to Information Desk, and train graduate students to sit at the desk and answer directional and short-answer queries while referring research questions to on-call librarians or by appointment.[34]
- The reference interview continues to thrive in human-to-human interaction via e-mail and live chat.
- In a 2009 study of New Jersey academic science libraries, conventional reference desks were the norm augmented by online reference services.[35]
- That end users continue to ask real research reference questions and need a point of contact warrants maintaining a research help desk, an online presence, or something like it.

If nothing else, these challenging 64 death assertions and 50 life-affirming allegations of reference service and the reference interview show how librarians have little trouble deeply critiquing their profession. This little exercise supports the spirit of my answer to that old high school colleague. Let us return.

"So, Dave, what do you do?"

"I'm a librarian."

"Isn't everything available on the Internet? Why do we need libraries and librarians?"

"Well, that's a fair question and one I get asked from time to time. Let me ask you a question. When you're using your tablet or mobile phone to find something you really need to know, do you think what you find is true?"

"Now that you mention it, sure I wonder about that, or if it's some weird conspiracy thing, or if I'm looking at something . . . I figure someone else can probably see what I'm doing. That's just creepy."

"Libraries and librarians can be trusted. They were made by folks like you who wanted to know that they could get a good answer and not worry if others knew. Let me ask you something else."

"Go ahead."

"How many full books can you find using your computer?"

"Oh, I dunno, maybe a million."

"Have you read any like that—on your computer?"

"Hell no! I might watch YouTube videos or read my e-mail for a couple of hours but not a whole book."

"Well, last I checked, not only do libraries have just about any book you might want to read, but they're free."

"That's true. I do like the feel of a book."

"Even if libraries were to disappear today, I think that some of the things librarians do best, like connecting people with information they want, will stay on in new and different ways. For example, did you know that you can click on a web link and get a live librarian in a couple of seconds, who'll answer a question about almost anything?"

"You mean, something like how I text my mom's caregiver to see how my mom's doing?"

"Yeah, something like that. Look, enough about me. What are you doing these days?"

"Oh, I'm a window washer up in the desert area. It may not sound fancy, but it pays the bills and I get to choose my own hours."

"Now that sounds stable. We'll always have windows to wash."

"LOL."

For continuing the conversation "Is the reference interview dead?" join me and others on my book blog, at http://referenceinterview.wordpress.com/.

## NOTES

1. William Miller, "What's Wrong with Reference? Coping with Success and Failure at the Reference Desk," *American Libraries* 15, no. 5 (1984): 303–6, 321.

2. Jerry D. Campbell, "Clinging to Traditional Reference Services: An Open Invitation to Libref.Com," *Reference and User Services Quarterly* 39, no. 3 (2000): 223–26.

3. Peter Hernon and Charles R. McClure, "Unobtrusive Reference Testing: The 55 Percent Rule," *Library Journal* 111, no. 7 (1986): 37–41.

4. Lara Bushallow-Wilbur, Gemma DeVinney, and Fritz Whitcomb, "Electronic Mail Reference Service: A Study," *RQ* (1996): 359–63.

5. Joseph Janes, "What Is Reference For?" *Reference Services Review* 31, no. 1 (2003): 22, 23, 25.

6. Catherine M. Robinson and Peter Reid, "Do Academic Enquiry Services Scare Students?" *Reference Services Review* 35, no. 3 (2007): 413, 414, 417, 418.

7. Susan M. Ryan, "Reference Transactions Analysis: The Cost-Effectiveness of Staffing a Traditional Academic Reference Desk," *Journal of Academic Librarianship* 34, no. 5 (2008): 389, 394, 398.

8. Marianne Stowell Bracke et al., "Finding Information in a New Landscape: Developing New Service and Staffing Models for Mediated Information Services," *College and Research Libraries* 68, no. 3 (2007): 248.

9. William L. Whitson, "Differentiated Service: A New Reference Model," *Journal of Academic Librarianship* 21, no. 2 (1995): 104–5.

10. Sara Tompson and Catherine Quinlan, "Reference Desk Renaissance: Connecting with Users in the Digital Age," *ACRL* (March 30–April 2, 2011): 369, 371, 372. http://0-www.ala.org.catalog.wblib.org/acrl/sites/ala.org.acrl/files/content/conferences/confsandpre-confs/national/2011/papers/reference_desk.pdf.

11. Martha Kyrillidou and Les Bland, eds., *ARL Statistics 2007–2009* (Washington, DC: Association of Research Libraries, 2009), 8. http://publications.arl.org/ARL-Statistics-2008-2009.

12. Keith Ewing and Robert Hauptman, "Is Traditional Reference Service Obsolete?" *Journal of Academic Librarianship* 21, no. 1 (1995): 3.

13. Christy R. Stevens, "Reference Reviewed and Re-envisioned: Revamping Librarian and Desk-Centric Services with LibStARs and LibAnswers," *Journal of Academic Librarianship* 39, no. 2 (2013): 202, 203, 205–7.

14. Cheryl LaGuardia, "The Future of Reference: Get Real!" *Reference Services Review* 31, no. 1 (2003): 40.

15. Thelma Freides, "Current Trends in Academic Libraries," *Library Trends* 31, no. 3 (1983): 467.

16. Sara Davidson and Susan Mikkelsen, "Desk Bound No More: Reference Services at a New Research University Library," *Reference Librarian* 50, no. 4 (2009): 347.

17. Barbara Ford, "From Discussion to Action: Changing Reference Service Patterns," *Journal of Academic Librarianship* 18, no. 5 (1992): 285.

18. Miller, "What's Wrong with Reference?" 304–6.

19. Campbell, "Clinging to Traditional Reference," 224–26.

20. Janes, "What Is Reference For?" 22–25.

21. Robinson and Reid, "Do Academic Enquiry Services Scare Students?" 418, 419, 421.

22. Ryan, "Reference Transactions Analysis," 395, 397, 398.

23. Russell F. Dennison, "Usage-Based Staffing of the Reference Desk: A Statistical Approach," *Reference and User Services Quarterly* 39, no. 2 (1999): 165.

24. Lee W. Hisle, "Reference Questions in the Library of the Future," *Chronicle of Higher Education* 52, no. 6 (2005), B7.

25. Hisle, "Reference Questions in the Library," B6.

26. Tompson and Quinlan, "Reference Desk Renaissance," 371, 372.

27. Jack O'Gorman and Barry Trott, "What Will Become of Reference in Academic and Public Libraries?" *Journal of Library Administration* 49, no. 33 (2007): 329.

28. Scott Carlson, "Are Reference Desks Dying Out?" *Chronicle of Higher Education* 53, no. 33 (2007): A38.

29. Brian Mathews, "While Reference Stats Decline, Oregon Surges +51%: A Glimpse at Some ARL Outliers," *The Ubiquitous Librarian* (blog), http://theubiquitouslibrarian.typepad.com/the_ubiquitous_librarian/2008/12/while-reference-stats-decline-oregon-surges-51-a-glimpse-at-some-arl-outliers.html.

30. Marie L. Radford and Scott Vine, "An Exploration of the Hybrid Reference Service Model: Keeping What Works," in *Reference Reborn: Breathing New Life into Public Services Librarianship*, ed. Diane Zabel (Santa Barbara, CA: Libraries Unlimited/ABC Clio, 2011), 79.

31. Stevens, "Reference Reviewed and Re-envisioned," 206–8.

32. LaGuardia, "The Future of Reference," 40.

33. John W. Fritch and Scott B. Mandernack, "The Emerging Reference Paradigm: A Vision of Reference Services in a Complex Information Environment," *Library Trends* 50, no. 2 (October 15, 2001): 294–95.

34. Stephanie J. Schulte, "Eliminating Traditional Reference Services in an Academic Health Sciences Library: A Case Study," *Journal of the Medical Library Association* 99, no. 4 (2011): 273–74.

35. Patricia H. Dawson, "Are Science, Engineering, and Medical Libraries Moving Away from the Reference Desk? Results of a Survey of New Jersey Libraries," *Science and Technology Libraries* 30, no. 4 (2011): 352.

*Chapter Two*

# A Literature Review of the Reference Interview

In an effort to provide a frame of reference, a brief introductory review of selected sources on the reference interview is provided in two parts. In part 1, the concept is searched and analyzed for its comprehensive coverage in three bibliographic content sources: Online Computer Library Center's WorldCat, Thomson Reuters' Citation Indexes, and Google's Google Scholar. In part 2, a selection of reference interview articles is evaluated under three broad types: literature reviews, anecdotal observations, and inferential studies. This literature review does not include coverage of the reference interview as it exists in blogs, wikis, video sharing, podcasts, social networking, and so on. However, these mediums and others are covered in my book blog at http://referenceinterview.wordpress.com/.

## PART 1: THREE BIBLIOGRAPHIC SOURCES CONSULTED

### WorldCat

WorldCat is the world's largest database of mostly the holdings data (libraries that hold the title) of books and journals/magazines representing more than 2 billion items globally.[1] In searching by keyword in WorldCat for the phrase *"reference interview*"* (employing the phrase-building quotation marks and the asterisk truncation symbol to include *interview, interviews,* and *interviewing*), there were 437 results; for *"reference transaction*"* there were 103; and for *question negotiation** there were 51 (August 10, 2013). The terms appeared in such fields as the title and the table of contents. *Question negotiation,* an important subset of the reference interview, was included in this review because of its perceived essential holdings in the literature.

Unfortunately, none of these expressions are indexed as a part of the Library of Congress's controlled vocabulary, such as subject headings, except for the single corporate name *Midwest Health Science Library Network, Reference Interview Project Team,* as part of the library's name authority file. To be fair, the closest Library of Congress subject headings seem to be the broader-controlled authority terms of *Reference services (Libraries)— Study and teaching* or *Library technicians—Training of* or even the single heading *Interviewing,* all of which are not addressed in this analysis because they are not narrow enough.

If one gauges popularity and maybe usefulness by a book's holdings, the title that is collected at the most number of institutions, with 1,331 holdings, is Bopp and Smith's 1995 *Reference and Information Services: An Introduction* (second edition).[2] Coming in second place, with 1,240 holdings, is McDaniel and Ohles's 1993 *Training Paraprofessionals for Reference Service: A How-to-Do-It Manual for Librarians.*[3]

Adding the results of the three keyword phrases *"reference interview\*"* (437), *"reference transaction\*"* (103), and *"question negotiation\*"* (51), a total of 591 items, pales somewhat when compared to the search results of the broader concept library *reference* (keyword as phrase "library reference" results in 7,800 for all items). Nevertheless, these preliminary findings indicate that the 591 reference interview–type titles are relatively few and somewhat dated, with (at least the top two books) how-to-do-it content and introductory material focusing on best practices.

## Citation Indexes

The second bibliographic source consulted was Thomson Reuters' Citation Indexes (using its Web of Science database), which indexes the most internationally respected research journals with high impact factors in a number of disciplines. A journal's impact factor represents the average number of other works that cite recent articles of that journal. The claim is that a measure of a journal's importance is its higher impact factor number. For this reason, a search of Citation Indexes would provide a sense of the dispersion of the reference interview topic within scholarly, high-impact journals. A *Topic* field indicator search yielded 199 results for the search string *"reference interview\*"* OR *"reference transaction\*"* OR *"question negotiation\*"* in *Science Citation Index, Social Sciences Citation Index,* and *Arts & Humanities Citation Index* (August 11, 2013). A search using the *Topic* field indicator includes title, abstract, and author generated keyword fields.

A long-standing industry standard in citation tracking, Citation Indexes report the number of times that a journal article is cited in other Citation

Indexes journals. From the resulting 199 articles found in the aforementioned search string, 4 titles have been cited by 50 or more Citation Indexes sources, which give some indication of the articles' importance on the topic and the writing skill of the authors, evidence perhaps toward gaining them some kind of rock-star status of the profession. Those 4 articles, their authors, and number of resources that cited them in Citation Indexes are as follows:

- Taylor's 1968 "Question-Negotiation and Information-Seeking in Libraries," cited by 364, a comparatively large number.[4]
- Dervin and Dewdney's 1986 "Neutral Questioning: A New Approach to the Reference Interview," cited by 83.[5]
- Wang and Soergel's 1998 "A Cognitive Model of Document Use during a Research Project," cited by 82.[6]
- Lynch's 1978 "Reference Interviews in Public Libraries," cited by 51.[7]

The 4 most cited articles in Citation Indexes indicate that scholarly dissemination has been covered on the topic since at least 1968 and that these discussions include question negotiation, information-seeking behavior, neutral questioning, cognitive modeling, and reference interviews.

An analytical tool that comes with Thomson Reuters' Web of Science search interface provides the frequency of these articles by journal title. Of the 199 article manuscripts, 60 (30 percent) were published in one journal, the *Reference User Services Quarterly* and its former title, *Reference Quarterly*. The three journals holding the next-most number of these 199 articles were *College Research Libraries*, with 15 (7.5 percent); the *Journal of Academic Librarianship*, also 15 (7.5 percent); and *Library Quarterly*, with 10 (5 percent). Of the 199 articles, the author contributing toward the most number of articles was Dewdney (8), followed by Pomerantz (6), Ross (6), and Shachaf (5). As a comparison to the aforementioned three-term search string, in a *Topic* field search the number of results for the term *library reference* generated 7,497 items and, when searched as the phrase *library reference*, 140.

## Google Scholar

The third and final bibliographic source consulted was Google Scholar, the freely available search engine that indexes the full text of scholarly material, mostly books, articles, dissertations, and reports. Because the three bibliographic sources consulted are different by both content and ability to limit results, no exact comparison of the three was attempted. Nevertheless, results from Google Scholar were made by applying the same quotation-mark technique as the other two, with both singular and plural forms of the three concepts in only the title filed. In addition, *citation entries* in Google Scholar,

usually duplicates of title searches, were not included. Under these parame-
ters, the title fields searched in Google Scholar resulted in 136 records for
*"reference interview,"* 23 for *"reference interviews,"* 29 for *"reference
transaction,"* 47 for *"reference transactions,"* 27 for *"question negotiation,"* and 1 for *"question negotiations"* (August 11, 2013). The total number of records in Google Scholar for all six *reference interview* terms in title
searches only came to 263.

Google Scholar has a similar citation feature as found in Citation Indexes,
noted by the link *cited by*, followed by a number, representing the number of
resources indexed in the Google Scholar database that have cited the item. As
previously noted, *cited by* amounts are one indication of the importance of a
resource. From the title search of the three concepts and their plurals, 4
articles are cited by more than 100 other sources. Three of the top 4 articles
are the same discovered in Citation Indexes—namely, Taylor, cited by 979
(in Google Scholar); Dervin and Dewdney, cited by 236; and Lynch, cited by
109. The fourth article is E. G. Abels' 1996 "The E-Mail Reference Interview," cited by 140 (again in Google Scholar), which also showed up in
Citation Indexes results but not until the 10th entry and cited by 31 sources.[8]
The results from Google Scholar appear to confirm what was discovered in
Citation Indexes, specifically, similar totals of unique titles on the topic (263
and 199) and 3 of the same most-cited journal articles. One difference between these two citation sources is the larger number of Google Scholar's
citations that can be attributed to the higher criteria of scholarly rigor for
journals indexed by Citation Indexes.

## PART 2: A LITERATURE REVIEW OF THE REFERENCE INTERVIEW UNDER THREE TYPES

Continuing with a review of a selection of article literature on the reference
interview, the published corpus of studies can be categorized and discussed
under three general types: literature reviews, anecdotal observations, and
inferential statistical studies.

### Literature Reviews

In the category of literature review, one of the most ambitious is Bunge's
impressive 1984 "Interpersonal Dimensions of the Reference Interview: A
Historical Review of the Literature," with 94 cited references.[9] He has
wielded significant influence in reference scholarship on his own accord,
particularly in the state of Wisconsin, as well as with his work in the
American Library Association. In this work, he furthered the professional
groundings of the reference interview—both its history and its praxis. He

was one of the first to acknowledge the documented early date of 1876 for the humble beginnings of modern reference work.

In significant contrast to Bunge's seminal work is Luo's 2007 "Chat Reference Competencies: Identification from a Literature Review and Librarian Interviews."[10] Luo's piece is indicative of the reference interview's ability to adapt toward new modalities in the early part of the twenty-first century—in this case, synchronous chat reference. Highlighting a handful of recent articles and books on chat reference competencies (mostly 2002–2006), the author's unique contribution for this fledgling and popular reference service is her thirteen categories of best practices and the summary of competencies in the discussion section that follows.

With the risk of breaking with decades of scholarly tradition, this next bibliography covering the reference interview was included in part because of its English abstract and works cited (i.e., not its full text). Nozomi's "Approaches in the Studies of Reference Process and Its Integration: Focusing on the Studies of Reference Interviews" is in Japanese (an English version was anticipated but not delivered using interlibrary loan); nevertheless, it is clearly contributing something significant from a different perspective.[11] This literature review builds a conceptual framework on the term *reference process*, a term inclusive of the reference transaction and the reference interview. For this reason, all the articles chosen are studies of the reference process divided into three groups: empirical studies, studies from the interactional point of view (evaluating learning as an outcome of interaction between librarian and patron), and studies from the cognitive point of view (librarian's knowledge during the reference process).

Finally, I would be negligent if I did not mention Richardson's 2002 "The Current State of Research on Reference Transactions."[12] In this fifty-five-page, part-narrative, part-annotated bibliography, the author reviews, in a chronological, systematic style, upward of ninety works on the reference transaction dating from 1926 through 2002. Although most of the literature on the reference transaction is predictably descriptive and anecdotal, the articles reviewed by Richardson all follow an analytical approach. For example, Conner's 1927 research collected 24,727 reference inquiries at the Carnegie Library of Pittsburgh in four-month periods during the years 1905, 1910, 1915, 1920, and 1925.[13] Using the Dewey classification scheme in a cross-tabulation technique, she was able to reveal broad subject trends: first sociology, then history, and finally literature. On the other end of the twentieth century, Saxton's 1997 meta-analysis of twelve reference accuracy studies found a correlation between seven variables (e.g., library expenditures, number of added volumes, size of population served) and reference answer accuracy.[14]

## Anecdotal Observations

The second of three types of article literature of the reference interview falls under anecdotal observations. These types of articles are often labeled secondary-class citizens of the research community, even questionable. There are legitimate reasons for this bias, but for the current literature review, anecdotal observations mean those published contributions to the reference interview practice that take a constructive critical approach to an experience model that informs toward better behaviors for the reference staff. This part of the review is to be viewed as advice from seasoned veterans: advice designed to improve the interview experience and the art, if you will, of fielding patrons' questions with outcomes of accuracy, usefulness, and a high degree of user satisfaction.

Three examples are presented here in an attempt to represent the diverse spectrum of published anecdotal observations of the reference interview: cross-disciplinary adaption, theoretical building, and descriptive analysis. The first case, Radcliff's provocative 1995 "Interpersonal Communication with Library Patrons: Physician-Patient Research Models," takes an old idea and connects it to a new dot. This work is in the category of adapting ideas from other disciplines for the reference interview. Grounded in communication theory and its well-documented science, it takes an old common interaction—that between doctor and patient—and extracts observable constructs that are similar to librarian-patron conversations that could inform a better practice of the interview.[15] The process between physician and patient leading to a successful cure is similar to an accurate answer response in a librarian's question negotiation session. The change in normal of the physician-patient relationship over the years, from a dominant-passive one to a more shared power role, provides an interesting paradigm shift for the librarian-patron relationship, especially in light of disintermediation (i.e., patrons finding information on their own without the help a mediator/librarian).

The second example or type of anecdotal observation demonstrating diversity in this part of the literature is also the second article discovered in the Citation Indexes search: Dervin and Dewdney's 1986 "Neutral Questioning: A New Approach to the Reference Interview."[16] This work fits in the category of constructing theories for the reference interview. This blockbuster, game-changing article (if I may be so bold) is a mere seven pages long but is backed up by thirteen years of thoughtful reading, observing, surveying, and serious construction of a theory called *sense making*. In brief, the idea of neutral questioning is grounded in the conceptual framework (like an architect's drawing plans for a house) of sense making, where the end users are stopped but desire to continue to move through, to make sense of (if you will), a gap in their path toward gaining the information they seek. Neutral questioning is a technique that emerged out of sense-making theory, a theory that the authors intended to apply in contexts beyond just the field of library and information science. Unfortunately, this type of grounding an idea in a theory is seriously lacking in anecdotal published studies.

The third and final example of a type of anecdotal observation is Hammill and Fojo's 2013 "Using Secret Shopping to Assess Student Assistant Training."[17] This is in the category of an analysis of results relying on descriptive information only, often summarized in charts or tables and frequently the study of one's own reference services. Perfected in the field of market research, secret shoppers typically purchase in an assigned retail location and report back observations for the sake of improvement. In Hammill and Fojo's work, the practice was applied to establish if their library's circulation student workers were giving incorrect reference advice and to improve student training in this area. The results and analysis were based on secret shoppers' answers to a questionnaire filled out after their experience. Data included summary of conversations and eleven tables of descriptive information, such as questions asked, time of interaction, and enthusiasm (based on a five-point Likert scale). Analysis found some bias on the part of the shoppers (which skewed the data), the redrafting of the questionnaire parts for subsequent rounds 2 and 3, and that the practice of handing out librarian business cards and patrons filling out reference question forms does not work.

## Inferential Statistical Studies

Continuing with the criteria of a selection of articles divided by three types, the third and last category for the reference interview is inferential statistical studies. Simply put, these studies all use some form of analysis that infers or makes a prediction about a population based on a representative sample of that population. Because of the comprehensive contribution to this part of the literature up through 2002 by Richardson in his "Current State of Research on Reference Transactions,"[18] what follows is a sampling of articles from 2003 through 2013.

The succeeding three dimensions of the reference interview from articles utilizing inferential statistics are proposed: a focus on the reference provider, a focus on the end user, and miscellaneous. An example of an article centering on the reference provider in this way is Wu and Liu's 2003 "Intermediary's Information Seeking, Inquiring Minds, and Elicitation Styles."[19] The study included the recording and transcribing of thirty patron-intermediary reference transactions with a total of five intermediaries at five separate institutions to identify Mandarin Chinese utterances and elicitations (speech sequences). Chi-square was applied to analyze the elicitation frequencies of the five intermediaries. Statistically significant differences were discovered among all five intermediaries in light of three concepts: forms, purposes, and functions. These results highlight the complexity of communication that takes place during the reference interview.

An example of the second type of an inferential statistical article, where the focus is on the end user, is Khosrowjerdi and Iranshahi's 2011 study "Prior Knowledge and Information-Seeking Behavior of PhD and MA students."[20] Pearson correlation tests were applied in two of three hypotheses, showing a positive relationship between prior knowledge (e.g., experience in using a source) and information-seeking behavior (easier, faster searching performances) of MA and PhD students. A *t* test for a third hypothesis found no significant differences in means between groups of men and women and PhD/MA students.

An example of the third and final type of an inferential statistical article—labeled *miscellaneous* because these studies do not explicitly measure the reference provider nor the end user—is Dubnjakovic's 2012 "Electronic Resource Expenditure and the Decline in Reference Transaction Statistics in Academic Libraries."[21] Using multiple regression analysis and general linear modeling, Dubnjakovic analyzed three expenditure variables (e-books, computer hardware, and bibliographic utility costs collapsed into one mean variable) and reference transaction data (including face-to-face, phone, e-mail, chat) from 3,925 respondents of the biannual 2006 Academic Library Survey. Findings showed that an increase in spending on electronic resources increased the number of reference transactions in a typical week.

This two-part literature review of mostly reference interview articles provides a brief overview of how the topic has been covered in the field of published sources. In part 1, after a comprehensive search in three popular bibliographic content sources, it was determined that there are no less than 263 works on the reference interview. Part 2 divides the literature of the topic into three types of categories—namely, literature reviews, anecdotal observations, and inferential statistical studies. The spectrum of works ran from comprehensive bibliographies noting the earliest published mention of reference services (1876) to rock-star, game-changing pieces backed by more than a decade of reflection. It is hoped that this small contribution to the review of the reference interview will inspire forthcoming scholars to continue to test the past, practice well in the present, and imagine a future of best practices that will contribute to a successful, sustainable vocation of library and information professionals.

## NOTES

1. Online Computer Library Center, "2,000,000,000 Holdings and Growing . . . ," http://www.oclc.org/en-US/worldcat.html.

2. Richard E. Bopp and Linda C. Smith, *Reference and Information Services: An Introduction*, 2nd ed. (Englewood, CO: Libraries Unlimited, 1995).

3. Julie Ann McDaniel and Judith K. Ohles, *Training Paraprofessionals for Reference Service: A How-to-Do-It Manual for Librarians* (New York: Neal-Schuman, 1993).

4. Robert S. Taylor, "Question-Negotiation and Information Seeking in Libraries," *College and Research Libraries* 29, no. 3 (1968): 178–94.

5. Brenda Dervin and Patricia Dewdney, "Neutral Questioning: A New Approach to the Reference Interview," *Reference Quarterly* 25, no. 4 (1986): 506–13.

6. Peiling Wang and Dagobert Soergel, "A Cognitive Model of Document Use during a Research Project: Study I. Document Selection," *Journal of the American Society for Information Science* 49, no. 2 (1998): 115–33.

7. Mary Jo Lynch, "Reference Interviews in Public Libraries," *Library Quarterly* 48, no. 2 (1978): 119–42.

8. Eileen G. Abels, "The E-Mail Reference Interview," *Reference Quarterly* 35, no. 3 (1996): 345–58.

9. Charles A. Bunge, "Interpersonal Dimensions of the Reference Interview: A Historical Review of the Literature," *Drexel Library Quarterly* 20, no. 2 (1984): 4–23.

10. Lili Luo, "Chat Reference Competencies: Identification from a Literature Review and Librarian Interviews," *Reference Services Review* 35, no. 2 (2007): 195–209.

11. Ikeya Nozomi, "Approaches in the Studies of Reference Process and Its Integration: Focusing on the Studies of Reference Interviews," *Library and Information Science* 30 (1992): 43, 58.

12. John V. Richardson, "The Current State of Research on Reference Transactions," *Advances in Librarianship* 26, no. 26 (2002): 175–230.

13. M. Conner, "What a Reference Librarian Should Know," *Library Journal* 52, no. 8 (1927): 415–18.

14. Matthew L. Saxton, "Reference Service Evaluation and Meta-analysis: Findings and Methodology Issues," *Library Quarterly* 67, no. 3 (1997): 267–89.

15. Carolyn J. Radcliff, "Interpersonal Communication with Library Patrons: Physician-Patient Research Models," *Reference Quarterly* 34, no. 4 (1995): 497, 498.

16. Dervin and Dewdney, "Neutral Questioning," 506, 507.

17. Sarah Jane Hammill and Eduardo Fojo, "Using Secret Shopping to Assess Student Assistant Training," *Reference Services Review* 41, no. 3 (2013): 8–18.

18. Richardson, "The Current State of Research," 222.

19. Mei-Mei Wu and Ying-Hsang Liu, "Intermediary's Information Seeking, Inquiring Minds, and Elicitation Styles," *Journal of the American Society for Information Science and Technology* 54, no. 12 (2003): 1117–33.

20. Mahmood Khosrowjerdi and Mohammad Iranshahi, "Prior Knowledge and Information-Seeking Behavior of PhD and MA Students," *Library and Information Science Research* 33, no. 4 (2011): 331–35.

21. Ana Dubnjakovic, "Electronic Resource Expenditure and the Decline in Reference Transaction Statistics in Academic Libraries," *Journal of Academic Librarianship* 38, no. 2 (2012): 94–100.

*Chapter Three*

# Scenario 1

*Virtual Reference: Less Is More*

Speaking from my limited perception, there is a common observation that reference librarians are too busy, with too much clutter, with too many responsibilities. We are a strange breed of generalists who, well, are addicted to learning (if that's so bad) and are more than happy, let's say very eager, to answer as carefully and precisely as we can a fairly wide spectrum of reference queries. We are rather proud of the idea that we have a proficiency birthed through library school (if not before), honed during those early attempts at the reference desk via phone, chat, e-mail, and so on, and, eventually, slowly, purposely, day by day groaning into a measure of . . . expertise. With this sometimes unappreciated (if we're honest) high level of knowledge, we reference librarians entertain a kind of entitlement attitude—that if we could just have a few more moments of time, we would find that elusive answer. Nevertheless, it does not come, and it does not come, and it does not come. Argh! Therefore, we finally throw down our smugness and say, "Ahem, I'm not finding a good answer for your question; I'll need to refer you on to another librarian." However, we should have done so fifteen minutes ago!

In contrast to this tendency to appeal to the patron—that, if given just a few more moments, we're certain to find their answer—is the view that simplicity and timeliness lead to good design. In other words, less is more. A concise reference interview is, all things being equal, better than a very long one. If one librarian is not getting at a correct answer in a reasonable time, the question is to be referred on to another.[1] The following scenario attempts to illustrate this "less is more" idea in a public library setting through an online chat exchange, where the librarian reflects on something learned in library school (imagine that). However, understand that this belief in brevity would not have hung around so long unless it had some measure of truth in it, a truth valid not only for one's life but, most assuredly, for the reference interview.

## THE SCENARIO

Being that it was my usual time for lunch, I was devouring one of those delicious BLT sandwiches that my wife packed for me, when I heard a ping from my laptop: "Patron Arrive." With twenty-seven other virtual reference librarians online at that moment—some public (such as myself) and others academic—I rolled my mouse's cursor over the patron's name, Fred, and Fred's question appeared: "I'm a senior at West Side High and my teacher said I needed more primary articles for my assignment on cell biology. Articles should be from 2011 and 2012." There was no asterisk next to Fred's name—meaning that no one from his library was monitoring at that moment. He was up for grabs. I clicked on his name as I took one last bite of the BLT.

My monitor seemed to flicker slightly, then the right side of my screen morphed into the patron's question. I got him! As soon as his name appeared in my space, I began our conversation.

**Librarian 1:** Hi, Fred. I'm reading your question.

*My mind flashed back to Dr. Andrew McDougal's virtual reference course in library school. "Less 'n more" he reminded emerging reference librarians in his thick Scottish accent. "Don't keep the patron wait'n, keep your responses back to the patron to less 'n two minutes."*

*I'd been doing virtual reference for over two years. You'd think I'd get used to the rush that one feels at this point in the transaction. There was something about the newness of each question, the challenge to get it right quickly.*

**Patron:** Hello.

*I selected one of my personal scripts and waited a few more seconds before sending it on, giving the appearance that I'd just typed it.*

**Librarian 1:** I'm a reference librarian at Springfield Public Library in Southern California. We're part of a national virtual reference cooperative. So, I'm not at your school, but I can help you with your question.

**Patron:** OK.

*Five seconds later . . .*

**Patron:** So could you please tell me where I can find the primary articles?

*Fred's original query seemed complete enough, so I didn't ask him to clarify it. He also seemed to be in a hurry. I quickly checked Fred's library's policy page. The page revealed that visiting virtual librarians were not given guest log-ons and passwords. But I had access to the same science database through Springfield's library page. I was on it.*

**Librarian 1:** Open another browser. I'll suggest a database and possible subject headings. First, let's make sure you've brought up another browser and you're on your library's webpage at http://wwwgeenvalley/west/lmc.k12.pa.us/.

*I would have tried the chat system's co-browsing function, but I knew from past tries that his library reference chat consortium didn't seem to support it very well. Maybe the next patron's would.*

*As I brought up Springfield's library page I continued . . .*

**Librarian 1:** Then go to "Find Articles."

**Patron:** I'm on that page now.

**Librarian 1:** OK great: now I suggest you scroll down and click on Science Abstracts.

**Patron:** OK, I did. Are science abstracts primary?

**Librarian 1:** I would consider them primary.

**Librarian 1:** OK, in the first search box, type "cell biology," then select "Subject" for the field to search. Then limit the date by typing "2011-2012" in the date box. Also, click on the drop-down menu on the bottom of the search screen and check "sort by date," so you get the most recent articles at the top of your results.

**Librarian 1:** Now, unless I'm mistaken, this database does have full text. But if not, you can click on the link at the bottom of each record that says "Find full text in another database," and it should link to the full text in another database from your library.

*My eyes paused on the bottom right-hand side of my computer screen. A minute and a half had passed.*

**Librarian 1:** Fred, how are you doing? Are you able to follow this?

*It's the hardest moment in a virtual librarian's life. Years of library school, as well as face-to-face and online reference practice, all come down to the next few seconds as they t-i-c-k-a-w-a-y. The green dot next to "Fred" let me know that he was still there, lurking.*

*Two minutes passed, then . . .*

**Patron:** OK.

*Two more minutes passed. My heart almost stops.*

**Patron:** I found some articles.

*Those must be some of the most beautiful words in a virtual librarian's world.*

**Patron:** But let me look them over first, so I can tell you if they are the ones I need.

*I took a deep breath. Placing my hand on the keyboard and . . .*

**Librarian:** OK, no problem. Take your time. I'll stay on.

**Patron 1:** Thank you.

*Four minutes pass. I begin to think about peeking at my e-mail (should I?) or clicking on another patron (I shouldn't).*

**Patron:** Hi, I found some articles that are related to my subject. But if I need further help, should I contact you?

*Twenty-five seconds later, I continued . . .*

**Librarian 1:** Hi, Fred. Probably the best thing to do is go back to where you first logged on to "Chat with a Librarian." You'll get another librarian who can help you.

**Patron:** Thank you for your help.

*I clicked on one of the institution's "good-bye" scripted messages.*

**Librarian 1:** Thank you for using our "Chat with a Librarian" service. Good-bye.

The system posts the following message as the green button turns to red next to Fred's name.

**Patron:** Patron ended chat session.

*I set the resolution code to "Answered" and closed out the session. I resumed enjoying my BLT, listening for the next patron ping.*

## REFLECTIONS

### Knowledge

- Design a timeline of the main events in this reference interview.
- In three words, what is the main principle illustrated in this scenario?
- Determine the ratio of words typed by the librarian and those typed by Fred. For example, if the librarian typed 100 words and Fred typed 20 words, the ratio would be 10:2. If this were a typical reference interview chat, what does the ratio tell you about what to expect?

### Comprehension

- What is your interpretation of Fred's term *primary articles*?
- What else besides *primary article*s could you imagine that Fred's high school teacher probably wanted in these articles?
- Write something about the ratio of words typed by the librarian versus those typed by Fred.

### Application

- What would be different about the librarian's response if Fred needed articles on Elaine Fuchs instead of cell biology?
- What other life events can you suggest use the *more is less* motif?
- In what ways would this reference interview have been different if Fred had asked his question face-to-face at the public library reference desk? On the phone?

### Analysis

- What was the pivotal moment in this reference interview and why?

- The high school senior, Fred, appeared to be rushed. What could you say to convince a skeptical librarian (who believes student patrons should never be spoon-fed their requests) that sometimes it is appropriate to do the work for the patron, with little or no information literacy instruction?
- Identify three things that Fred could have said more clearly so that the librarian could better answer his question.

## Synthesis

- Draw a simple flowchart showing how the librarian answered Fred's question.
- Write out your feelings about Fred. Write out your feelings about the librarian.
- What would happen differently if the co-browsing function worked and the librarian had access to the username and password for Fred's library databases?

## Evaluation

- In what ways did the librarian answer Fred's question completely or incompletely (choose one)?
- Pretend that you are this reference librarian's supervisor and have read the transcript created from this transaction. In your evaluation report on this reference interview, what would you note were good points, and what would you point out as areas for improvement?
- Go to the book's blog at http://referenceinterview.wordpress.com/, click on the link for this chapter (Scenario 1—Virtual Reference: Less Is More), and post a brief review of this chapter.

## NOTES

Originally published in *Reference Librarian* in 2007: Dave Harmeyer, "Virtual Reference: Less Is More," *Reference Librarian* 48, no. 1 (2007): 113–16.

1. See chapter 16, "A Conceptual Model for Online Chat Reference Answer Accuracy," for statistical significance demonstrating that less is more is quite true.

## Chapter Four

# Scenario 2

*A Phone Interview: Save the Time of the Reader*

I personally don't believe that it's unhealthy to think about your work during moments when you're not supposed to be working. I haven't passed this by Dr. Phil, but one indication that your job is probably a good fit is that you wake up in the middle of the night with an answer to a work problem, or, hmmm, maybe you remember that you forgot to turn in your annual report (ah, but that's the other side, not a good fit). Anyway, the librarians I know who are passionate about reference and its interview are generally thinking of new ways to do it better. I find myself daydreaming, of sorts, about my most recent reference interviews—how they went, how to make them work even better the next time—and so this book about reality scenarios by a real librarian has come to pass.

One area that often eludes me is how to save time in the reference transaction process or, in the words of a famous library professor from India, Ranganathan (more on him later), save the time of the reader.[1] I don't think that I'm merely suggesting to shorten the time of the interviews but to be brief about what is shared with the end users to reduce anxiety, motivate them toward being self-reliant researchers, and help save them time when they become more information compliant on their own. For example, would it be better for person $X$ if I focused on scholarly resources when the assignment actually calls for information on a current event? With the significant increase in adult learners in higher education, we have end users with a framework very different from that of the traditional undergraduate. They are busy adults who often have families and wonder how crazy it is to go back to school after twenty years and finish their degrees.

One method is to deal with these academic heroes (in my thinking) within the context of their often overwhelming lives. Other librarians might scold me and insist that our patrons fit our schedules—that they set up appointments, where there are fewer interruptions—not the other way around! Well, I beg to differ. The reward is not in schedules, my friend, but in changed lives, lives enriched by learning how to manage the workings of a democratic information society and—you may have guessed it—through adult learners' own information competency, caught during the most remarkable, messy time of their lives. I trust that the following scenario illustrates this to some degree—that is, by providing excellent reference service just in time, at the moment of need, and, in this case, to higher education's relatively new, growing undergraduate student population: the degree completion adult learner.[2]

## THE SCENARIO

I'd come fifteen minutes early to Brett College's [pseudonym] fifth and final faculty meeting of the year. I carefully sliced a sesame-seed bagel in two before smothering it in cream cheese, and I occasionally sipped black coffee sprinkled with three packages of sweetener. As fellow faculty members quietly trickled into the school's dimly lit theater, which doubled as our meeting room, my eyes bounced about the brightly lit sets onstage, which were poised for the coming week's final student productions.

I could just make out the words of the college choir, in the belly of a nearby room, finishing its rehearsal of the piece that we would soon hear.

"Ezekiel saw de wheel way up in de middle of de air . . . "[3]

As their words began to fade from my ears, my mind slowly awakened to a phone conversation that I'd had with a graduate student the day before. It was the final hour of a very packed day, and she was asking a reference question.

I answered the phone, "Brett College Library, this is Dave."

"Hi Dave, this is Sonja Martinez. Can I ask you to help me some more on my lit review?" she asked.

"Sure, just a moment," I said in as friendly a voice as possible.

Positioning my face in front of my glowing laptop screen, I moved my cursor and clicked the corner of the e-mail window, closing it. Trying to forget about responding to twenty last e-mails, I clicked open a new browser. It automatically opened to the library's hundred-plus database page.

Sonja had come by my office a week earlier, looking for help in getting started on her major project. She was a member of a cadre of twenty-three adult learners going through the school's very popular master's in organizational leadership program. Sonja was a bright Hispanic woman in her early thirties with short, jet-black hair. She was a part-time aerobics instructor at a local gym, part-time student at Brett, and full-time mom with two young children. She had her cell phone earpiece on and was making dinner.

"I'm fixing spaghetti tonight. Hope you don't mind that I work on it as we talk," said the fast-talking multitasker.

"Umm, sure. How can I help you?"

At that moment, I could hear the objections of my more cautious librarian colleagues advising, "Dave, you should control the moment and insist on a formal appointment to salvage the respectful attention required for a successful reference outcome." But I was also thinking of Ranganathan's fourth precept: save the time of the reader.

Sonja continued, "Thanks for meeting with me a week ago. I've got a much better handle on my topic—the effects of high-fructose corn syrup on weight gain. But I need some articles to back up my theory before I propose a research method. Do you have any ideas?"

"Hmm, yes. Do you remember our talk about controlled vocabulary?"

"Oh, you mean subject headings?"

"Yeah, library catalogers and those who index journal articles select terms to represent the content in articles and books. In theory, articles or books on your topic should be represented by a similar term or group of terms. Knowing your topic's subject headings will save you time and get you relevant articles and books for your lit review."

Just then, I could hear Sonja whispering, "Sweetheart, what is it? Mommy's on the phone. Yes, that's a lovely picture of an elephant." Her voice increased in volume. "Sorry, my four-year-old had to show me her latest work of art."

"No problem, Sonja," I responded. "That reminds me how earlier this morning my three-year-old Vicki climbed up on my lap and with sleepy eyes looked into my face to announce, 'Elephant begins with the letter L.'

"And then I said, 'No sweetie, elephant begins with the letter E. Ummm, you see, E has two sounds, E like in easy and E like in elephant.' But you know what; she wasn't convinced at all because she announced, 'No, Daddy, elephant starts with an L, L-e-phant!' Oh, well."

A grin broke over my face as I heard Sonja laughing on the other end of the phone.

I continued, "OK, back to your question. I'm pulling up a database that will likely have some articles for your topic."

"How do you know what database to go to?"

"Good question. Our databases are basically two kinds: discipline specific—like education or psychology—and general. Your topic would roughly fall into the food science area, but we don't have any food science databases. So, I suggest we look at one of the library's general databases."

Sonja interrupted, "Just a second. My spaghetti water is boiling; let me turn it down. And the meat sauce is now simmering on low. Let me go over to our computer."

I could hear Sonja put down a spoon, walk a few steps, and then whisper to her son, "Honey, mommy needs to use the computer." I could make out some mild frustration from a young boy and clearly heard a cartoon-like voice say, "Farmer Jud wants to play more another time. Goooood bye!"

In a couple of moments, Sonja continued, "OK, I'm on Brett's website; tell me where I go now."

As I directed her to the library's list of proprietary databases, I couldn't help but think how important it was to help students (yes, even adult learners) grow toward some level of information literacy: teaching patrons to fish, not just throw them a fish. But under the current circumstances, would I have the time? Or more important, would she be teachable? I was thinking that I needed to take Sonja from what she knew to what she might not know and keep her engaged. So, I asked her, "What kind of research have you done so far?"

"Well, I Googled my topic and found this great article."

A few years back, I would have rolled my eyes, paused, and, with a voice of professionalism, stated my standard, "Hmm, so you searched Google for your topic. Well, you know, it's not the best place to find relevant, authoritative research." But nowadays I just listen to what the person brings to the table. It amazes me what golden nuggets one can find on the free Internet with a little novice effort.

I then asked, "OK, can you let me know the author and title and I'll bring it up on my screen?"

Sonja proudly read, "It has a URL printed on the right margin, www.jacn.org, and it's from the *Journal of American Clinical Nutrition*. The authors are Palmer and Black and the title is 'The Manufacturing and Applications of High Fructose Sugar.'" I went to the website, typed in the first author's name, and, sure enough, up came the PDF full-text version of the article. You know, after having seen thousands of such digital facsimiles of the original print version, you'd think I'd get used to it. Nevertheless, each time, I'm still somewhat awed how technology makes such quick-and-easy access so seamlessly possible.

I announced, "Right, I've got it on my screen. Looks pretty close to your subject matter, and it does appear to come from a peer-reviewed source." I scrolled through the nine-page article. It had a chemical structure of fructose, a diagram of a corn kernel, several tables, and a flowchart showing the process of turning cornstarch into high-fructose corn syrup.

She continued, "I was trying to find some of the articles listed in the Reference section but can't find any."

I quickly scrolled to the last page. "I think I can help you find some of these. Which ones look interesting?"

"Number 25, the one by McMullen," she answered.

"Well, you see the 'In:' on the first line. That means this citation is from a chapter in a book. The book is called *Nutritive Sweeteners,* and it's edited by Luer. Open up another browser, click on Library Catalog, and I'll show you how you can get it."

We both clicked on Brett's electronic catalog.

"We'll likely not have this title. But our catalog is connected to a network of thirty-five other academic libraries in the area that collectively hold about 8 million unique titles. We have a service that sends the books you request to the library in a two-day turnaround, and it costs you nothing. Not bad, huh?"

"Wow! I had no idea. This is so great. Now, show me how it's done."

I continued, "OK. Just click on author/title and type in one of the authors from the book and not the author from the article; so that would be Luer. Then type one word in the title, 'nutritive,' and click 'submit search.' When the next screen comes up, just click the button that says 'Connect Plus,' and you should see the record for this book come up from one or more of the other libraries."

In a few moments, the record was on both our screens. I next took her through some additional screens where she requested the book from one of four available schools.

"So, in two days you should get an e-mail that lets you know it's ready to pick up. Oh, if you look back at the citation, at the end, the numbers 83–108 are the page numbers for the chapter. If you need any other books or book chapters, simply follow what we just did. Any questions?"

"I see three other books I'd like to order. So, I can get those as well?"

"Sure, we have a limit of one hundred items for graduate students. And if for some reason, you can't find a book the way I showed, then you can get it through interlibrary loans for a small fee."

"What about the articles? I tried to find numbers 29 and 31, but I kept getting their citation information but no full text," she said.

"OK, that's what you'll get on the Internet, unreliable full text. Let's go to Journal Finder on the library's webpage. I see that number 29 is from a journal called *Corn Foods World.* Type this journal title into the box at the top."

"I did. And it looks like we have it."

I followed Sonya's path and saw that she was right. In a few moments, after drilling down through the journal's electronic back issues, we both had the full text of the article on our screens.

"Now, Sonja, I noticed that this article is twelve years old. Typically, you want articles that are not much more than three to five years old. To capture more current information about your topic, I'm going back to my first suggestion. Let's go to the webpage that lists all our databases. Click on 'A' and then bring up one of our general databases, called 'Academic Articles.' Let's see if we can find what this database uses as subject headings for your topic. Type in the box 'high fructose corn syrup.'"

"OK, there are 112 articles on my screen. Oh, on the left side, there is a list of subject headings."

"Yes, that's the same thing I retrieved, 112. Those headings represent the top ones found in all 112 of these records. Now, let's redo your search using subject headings that will get closer to your topic. How about 'corn syrup' and 'obesity,'" I suggested.

"Sounds good." A few moments later, "Wow, I get eight articles. These look great, and they are all in the last three years!"

I finished up. "Just two more things: I see that two of these eight are not full text in this database. If you go back to 'Journal Finder,' you can type in those titles and see if they are full text in another database or if we subscribe to them in paper. Also, these articles and your book chapters will have other references that you can follow up as potential resources for your lit review."

"Dave, thanks for your time. I'll call or stop by your office if I need more help. Oops, got to get back to the spaghetti. And yes, honey, you can have the computer back."

I quickly finished up by saying, "No problem, Sonja. Take care and I look forward to hearing how it goes."

The conversation quickly faded in the back of my mind. In front of me now was the campus choir, onstage and sharing the Negro spiritual . . .

> Ezekiel saw de wheel
> Way up in de middle of de air
> Ezekiel saw de wheel
> Way in de middle of de air
> De big wheel run by faith
> And de little wheel run by de grace o' God.
> A wheel in a wheel—
> Way in de middle of de air.

The sounds of the academy and the thoughts of a librarian . . . saving the time of the reader.

## REFLECTIONS

## Knowledge

- Make a list of similarities and differences between library patrons who are undergraduate science majors and patrons who are degree completion adult learners in an organizational leadership evening program.

- Based on what you learned in the first bullet, describe a reference interview with an undergrad and then an adult learner.
- Make one or more acrostics that can be useful in remembering how to effectively serve these two very different types of patrons.

## Comprehension

- Based on what you have learned about Sonja in the scenario, write in your own words (not words from the story) what you think are her information needs. Be as broad as you like.
- Make a cartoon strip showing the sequence of events in the scenario.
- Based on this scenario and your own knowledge, write a definition of *information competency.*

## Application

- If you received this call from Sonja, what different responses could you have given her?
- Let's say that Sonja e-mailed you instead of called. Compose a set of instructions that answers her information need.
- Make up a board game (yes, the kind you played when you were a kid) that illustrates the main ideas in this scenario.

## Analysis

- How would you explain to Sonja your search strategy if she did not have a computer at hand?
- Find online and distinguish at least two kinds of resources (their citations) that the librarian found for Sonja—for example, a book and a peer-reviewed article. Compare the two citations as if you had to explain them to an adult learner.
- Go to the blog of this book at http://referenceinterview.wordpress.com/, click on the area for this chapter (Scenario 2—A Phone Interview: Save the Time of the Reader), and post a questionnaire that Sonja would take to help the librarian answer her information needs.

## Synthesis

- Imagine how this reference interview would take place ten years into the future (different technologies, different expectations on the part of Sonja and the librarian, different access to information, different learning outcomes).

- Write a job description for this librarian based on the tasks that he has accomplished.
- Predict three things that will happen the next time Sonja and the librarian get together face-to-face.

## Evaluation

- Take the opinion that the librarian should have set an appointment with Sonja instead of trying to meet her need on the phone. What three compelling grounds would you have for your claim?
- Pretend you are this reference librarian's supervisor and you overhear this reference interview. In your evaluation report, what would you note were good points, and what would you point out are areas for improvement?
- Divide your mind into two debate teams. Team 1 has the opinion that the best way to serve the individual research needs of adult learners is to have them set appointments with the librarian. Team 2 has the opinion that the best way to serve the research needs of adult learners is to meet their needs as best as possible at the point of contact. Use the suggestions found in ProQuest's "Teacher Mini-debate Guide."[4]

## NOTES

Originally published in *Reference Librarian* in 2007: Dave Harmeyer, "A Phone Interview: Save the Time of the Reader," *Reference Librarian* 48, no. 2 (2007): 83–88.

1. Shiyali Ramamrita Ranganathan, *The Five Laws of Library Science* (New York: Asia, 1963), 9.

2. Jovita M. Ross-Gordon, "Research on Adult Learners: Supporting the Needs of a Student Population That Is No Longer Nontraditional," *Peer Review* 13, no. 1 (2011): 26.

3. "*Ezekiel Saw de Wheel*, a song which is in the public domain." Philip C. Baxa and M. William Krasilovsky, "*Dawson v. Hinshaw Music, Inc.*: The Fourth Circuit Revisits Arnstein and the Intended Audience Test," *Fordham Intellectual Property, Media and Entertainment Law Journal* 1, no. 2 (1991): 91.

4. "ProQuest's Teacher Mini-debate Guide," October 2007, http://www.proquestk12.com/productinfo/pdfs/MiniDebate_Teachers.pdf.

*Chapter Five*

# Scenario 3

*At the Reference Desk: Harry Potter and the Secrets of Hogwarts*

If I were Malcolm Gladwell, I'd probably call it the *tipping point.*[1] In reference interviews, there seems to be a point where it all comes together and when the wait, the unsuccessful search results, and the losing of the patron's confidence change in a moment at the sign of, well, the tipping point. In that moment of the interaction, not only do you know that what you see looks promising, but the patron gets it, too. That is why this part of the library profession—the reference transaction—is occasionally referred to as both a science and an art. The science is the collective technologies that make our heads spin, the centuries of information gathering and preserving, as well as the statistical analyses that inform the practice. The art is when a certain level of devotion to the science produces the patron's answer in magical ways, even with flair. In fact, when conducting a reference interview, I sometimes feel like . . . a magician. It can begin when I hear students moan about the hours they just spent in vain looking for something on their topics. It ends with a few clicks in the right places with dozens of peer-reviewed articles on their very topics miraculously appearing before their eyes. The real trick in such an approach is that at the end of the show, the students should have moved in a positive direction along a personal scale of information competency.

In light of teaching information literacy during the transaction, I'm supposed to be more like a guide on the side. The roles in an ideal situation include an engaged student and the facilitating guide. Of course, there is no guarantee that we play those roles well. The students will be distracted, will look at their smartphones, answer text messages, and even update their Facebook pages during the interview. How rude! The guide, under the right circumstances (which happens much more than we admit), is greatly tempted to turn into a sage on the stage (for the record: not the ideal). Maybe the reference librarian is more like a guide/sage or sage/guide, if you will, who during the interview figures that the student could not possibly find his or her way back to this absolutely perfect peer-reviewed article and so e-mails the full text to the student, including a copy of the citation in the assignment's required APA style! How then does information literacy and the student's growth in information competency survive under these reality TV–like roles? It goes back to the reference interview being a kind of art. If done well, the interview is a mash-up of, yes, documents sent to the student in e-mail but also directions for enabling Google Scholar to link to the university's licensed database articles, search strings discovered using a database's thesaurus with uppercase Boolean operators, and a YouTube link to a seven-minute video on how to redo the search that produced said results. This type of guide/sage/artist reference librarian is depicted in the following scenario with both the often-pleasant tipping point phenomena and the mash-up kind of delivery of resources.

## THE SCENARIO

It was my tenth spring at Brett College and the golden trumpet trees were in full bloom, standing like mystic sentinels outside the south entrance of the library. Small embossed labels on their trunks announced their botanical name, sounding like some Harry Potter spell: *Tabebvia chrysotricha*, poof! The Southern California sunshine opened a thousand luscious fragrances, matched by an amazing array of intricate floral designs exploding all over campus. The grounds crew had cast its enchantment yet again.

A student appointment was added to my day earlier that morning as I was crossing the library's main floor and its computer commons. Practically every student looked hypnotized by screens of Facebook and MySpace. Coming toward me was Professor Amy Clark with one of her students in tow. A week ago, I conducted a library workshop with her class of ten students who were taking a remedial freshman writing seminar. Amy's approach to the class was rather novel, focusing the writing-phobic freshmen on studying famous authors' own struggles and successes on writing, a kind of writer's personal view of best practices.

"Hey Dave, do you have a moment? Rachel and I are having a hard time finding resources for J. K. Rowling. Can you help?"

"Sure Amy," I said enthusiastically. "Nice to see you again, Rachel. What's your schedule look like today?"

"Thanks, Professor Harmeyer. I have a class in a few minutes bu-but, mmm, I'm free at 1:30 today," she said in a soft, sheepish voice.

"OK, 1:30 it is. See you then."

"Thanks Dave," echoed Amy. "See you around."

"No problem. Take care," I said picking up a piece of scratch paper and writing *1:30, Rachel, J. K. Rowling.*

As the clock moved toward 1:30, I began to think through a strategy for finding something useful on how the author of the Harry Potter series thought about her own writing. Maybe our two literature databases would have indexed a few of Rowling's interviews. Perhaps our online catalog or its borrowing network of thirty-seven area libraries would have a relevant book or two. And, of course, I'd give the free web a try. With such a great topic, I was bound to find something to inspire this would-be author.

At 1:25, I moved out to the reference desk and turned on its monitor and desktop computer. At a little after 1:30, I watched Rachel walk alone through the library's glass doors. She approached the reference desk.

"Hi, Rachel. Why don't you sit down, and let's see what we can find." I adjusted the monitor so that we could comfortably view the computer screen together.

"Tha-tha-thanks again, Professor Harmeyer. I ho-ho-hope I'm not bo-bo-bottering you," she stammered as she took a seat next to mine.

"Oh, just call me Dave," I assured her, as I realized she was painfully shy and felt a little self-conscious about her stuttering. Her speech impediment was only one of a couple of things making her first year at Brett a challenge. Like many Latinas, she was the first in her large family to attend a university. A few scholarships helped pay some of her tuition, but her family (at some sacrifice) was covering the bulk of costs, room, and board.

"Let's see, I believe your topic was J. K. Rowling, right?"

"Yes."

"What made you choose her as your author?"

"Well, sin-since fifth grade, I've been reading all the Po-Potter books. I'd save up all my allowance, so I could buy a copy the day the new one ca-ca-came out," she said with some effort.

"Wow, that's great. So you like reading."

"Ah huh."

"Well, let's see what we can find." I moved the mouse around to find the location of my cursor on the screen and then clicked on the ubiquitous blue Internet browser's icon. The library's main page came up.

"As you may remember in class, we got to this page by clicking on the word 'Libraries' on the bottom left of Brett's main page. I'd like to start our search with the two literature-type databases that are part of our more than one hundred online databases."

I knew that the databases came from internationally recognized vendors and felt sure that one or both should have something. The first came up quickly on the monitor, and we were soon in the J. K. Rowling section. After five minutes, we found the names and dates of Rowling's writings, her biography, some criticisms, and a summary of each Potter book but nothing about how she wrote her captivating stories.

"Hmm, nothing here. Let's look at the second one."

I clicked on the browser's homepage icon, and up came Brett's library page again. Soon, the other database was up, and we were again on an entry for J. K. Rowling. This time, the information was similar to the first, except there were 197 citations under "criticisms." I began to dip into a few of them that looked promising. Finally, one entry caught my eye. It was titled "Of Magic and Single Motherhood," from the provocative, tabloid-like online magazine *Salon*.[2] We were soon on the *Salon* website and reading the article together. It was an interview with Rowling with some good first-person accounts about her writing techniques. I was mildly disappointed. I'd hoped to have more than one place to go from these two databases. I certainly could have missed something, but we needed to move on.

"OK, I'll send this *Salon* article link to your e-mail, so you'll have something to start with." Rachel began to fidget and sigh and look at her watch. She was beginning to act disinterested and bored. I was thinking, "Oh no, I'm losing her." At that moment, something deep within my librarian's soul struck me. It had something to do with the philosopher librarian from India named Ranganathan and his five laws of library science.[3] I'd come to appreciate the post–World War II thinker's profound five-point rubric for the library profession since I first heard them in library school. His second law states, *every reader its book*. Rachel was the reader, and the information that she needed about Rowling was her book. I pushed on.

"Rachel, do you remember in class how I talked about those books that captured famous authors' ideas on how they write. There was one for William Faulkner that included his correspondence and interviews with others and another for Hemingway. One of those books is right over here." I got up and walked over to the third bookcase from the desk, searched for a medium-size blue-green book, and returned to the desk. "Here it is: *Conversations with William Faulkner*. It still has a few bookmarks that I left from last week. Listen to this." I turned to a note that had *Nobel Prize* scribbled on it and read, "Mr. Faulkner, what did you think when they told you that you had won the Nobel Prize?

"Faulkner: I was very surprised. I never imagined that things that I had written in the fury of my solitude would find an echo in so many human hearts."[4]

Next, I flipped to a second note that had *words* written on it and read again: "Question: How do you go about choosing your words?"

"Answer: In the heat of putting it down, you might put down some extra words. If you rework it and the words still ring true, leave them in."[5]

I continued, "What we need is a book like this one for Rowling. Let's see what our school's online catalog might have."

I clicked on "Library Catalog," chose "Keyword" before typing the words "conversations Rowling," and pushed "Enter." Our catalog showed no hits. Then I clicked on the tab that searches the thirty-seven shared libraries in the area. Two items appeared: a video and a book.

"Wow, look here," I said. "There's a book called *Conversations with J. K. Rowling.* You can borrow it for free and it only takes three days to get here."[6]

"Hah, th-that's amazing! Thanks professor, ah, I-I mean Dave." And she was soon filling out the online form to borrow it on the spot.

"So, now we've got two items. Let's try the free Internet and see if there's anything else out there." I Googled the words "Rowling interviews." As expected, 1.8 million results came up. One site that showed great possibility was something called "Accio Quote!" the largest archive of J. K. Rowling interviews on the web. I thought, "Hmm, that should do the trick" and clicked on the link. A search engine appeared.

"Now, let's try the terms 'interviews' and 'writing' in this search screen," I suggested. Soon 453 pages came up with the searched words highlighted in bold within each record summary.

Rachel's demeanor suddenly changed. She was sitting on the edge of her seat, eyes wide open. "This l-l-looks pretty good," she said as I clicked the first entry. It magically revealed the following text-based interview:

> The interviewer shared how much calmer the Harry Potter author looked when compared to three years earlier at their last interview together.
>
> Rolling replied, "But you saw me probably during the worst time. The last time you interviewed me was not a happy time. Writing Book Four was an absolute nightmare. I literally lost the plot halfway through. My own deadline was totally unrealistic. That was my fault because I didn't tell anyone. I just ploughed on, as I tend to do in life, and then I realized I had really got myself into hot water. I had to write like fury to make the deadline and it half killed me and I really was, oh, burnt out at the end of it. Really burnt out. And the idea of going straight into another Harry Potter book filled me with dread and horror. And that was the first time I had ever felt like that.
>
> I had been writing Harry for 10 years come 2000 and that was the first time I ever thought, Oh God, I don't want to keep going."[7]

"I'll send you the URL for this site. Do you think this is enough to get you started?" I asked, not quite sure if my apparent magic mediation would create a spark of interest.

"Dave, you do-do-don't know what a big relief this is for me. I-I've been struggling with my assignments this semester and was just about ready to give up. If I have more questions, I'll let you know. I've another class to get to. Thanks again. It's nice to have a friend in the library."

"No problem. I'm just glad to get you going in the right direction. Have a great day."

Rachel gathered her things and was soon out the doors of the library.

I couldn't help but imagine that I was hearing something as she passed under those majestic golden trumpet trees, playing an imaginary mystical fanfare, loud enough for heaven to hear: "Every reader its book, even for you, Rachel."

## REFLECTIONS

### Knowledge

- Make a simple flowchart (main points) of the reference interview between Rachel and the librarian.
- Describe some of the possible barriers that Rachel struggles with that could challenge a librarian who is attempting to teach her information literacy.
- What part of the reference interview disappointed the librarian, and what type of resources eventually met Rachel's information need?

### Comprehension

- From the experiences depicted in this scenario, write a twenty-word (or less) sentence describing the reference interview.
- Why was it important that the librarian drew a connection between Rachel and Ranganathan's second law of library science, *every reader its book*?
- What are one or two techniques that the librarian used to keep Rachel engaged in the reference interview?

### Application

- Take a collection of images from the Internet to illustrate in a collage one best practice that the librarian did during this scenario.
- Could this reference interview have occurred in a public library? Why or why not?
- Construct a rubric or set of instructions that you can use as a poster session at an American Library Association annual conference explaining at least five points that the librarian used with Rachel to conduct a successful reference transaction.

## Analysis

- What are some of the motives of the librarian as he began his reference interview with Rachel?
- Describe the tipping point in this scenario.
- What is the underlying theme of this interview? Explain.

## Synthesis

- Invent a web-based automatic service of the future that would meet Rachel's information needs without a live reference librarian.
- Zinio (http://www.zinio.com/www/) has decided to feature this scenario, recently published as the lead article in a popular magazine. Design a cover of this interview that will display on Zinio's main webpage.
- On a five-point proficiency scale (1 = *significantly below*, 5 = *significantly above*), rate the librarian's proficiency in conducting this reference interview, and give reasons why you chose that score.

## Evaluation

- Go to the blog for this book at http://referenceinterview.wordpress.com/, click on the area for this chapter (Scenario 3—At the Reference Desk: Harry Potter and the Secrets of Hogwarts), and post a better solution for this reference interview.
- How would you meet Rachel's reference needs if she were deaf?
- Devise three questions that Rachel could answer after the reference interview to determine if she is more information literate than before it.

## NOTES

Originally published in *Reference Librarian* in 2008: Dave Harmeyer, "At the Reference Desk: Harry Potter and the Secrets of Hogwarts," *Reference Librarian* 49, no. 1 (2008): 103–8.

1. Malcolm Gladwell, *The Tipping Point: How Little Things Can Make a Big Difference* (New York: Little, Brown, 2002).

2. Margaret Weir, "Of Magic and Single Motherhood [interview with J. K. Rowling]," *Salon* 31 (March 1999).

3. Shiyali Ramamrita Ranganathan, *The Five Laws of Library Science* (New York: Asia, 1963), 75.

4. M. Thomas Inge, ed., *Conversations with William Faulkner* (Jackson: University Press of Mississippi, 1999), 174.

5. Inge, *Conversations with William Faulkner*, 67.

6. Lindsey Fraser, *Conversations with J. K. Rowling* (New York: Scholastic, 2001).

7. Deborah Skinner and Lisa Bunker, "Accio Quote! The Largest Archive of J. K. Rowling Interviews on the Web," http://www.accio-quote.org/index.html.

## Chapter Six

# Scenario 4

## *Virtual in Vegas*

Virtual synchronous chat reference interviews, the subject of my 2007 dissertation,[1] is no longer a passing fad of the early twenty-first century but is certainly here to stay. In a limited survey ($n = 31$) at two universities in the spring of 2011, students were given the six choices for the reference interview: instant messenger (online chat), e-mail, telephone, text messaging, Skype video conferencing, and face-to-face. The majority of the respondents chose online chat for research (53 percent) and fact-type reference (60 percent).[2] Chat is not only convenient, almost instant, and high in usability for the end user but also has benefits for the reference librarian. In addition to capturing many aspects of the reference transaction—from full transcripts to the number of seconds transpired during the interview—chat can be monitored from any location in the world with a decent Internet connection and a laptop.

Some chat reference services devote reference staff to monitoring only their constituents. For others who share costs in a consortium, the librarians monitor one or more respective queues, which can include many other institutions. This allows the institution's patrons to have access to the service 24/7/365. It is more likely that the monitoring librarian will get patrons not from their pool of constituents but from other universities and (if not separated out) public libraries from across the United States and occasionally abroad. Therefore, the spectrum of questions can be broad. In the following scenario, two kinds of chat patrons are illustrated—a diminutive patron followed by the extreme, a *chatty* patron.

## THE SCENARIO

It was 37°F in Las Vegas, and my temperature was 101.6°F. We arrived at our hotel at exactly 7 pm. No one told me that it becomes rather chilly in the city of lights at Christmas time. Two months earlier, I started booking a flight for our family of four out of Southern California to visit relatives back east. But flight choices had dwindled and prices skyrocketed. When I expanded my online search to include airports within 300 miles, I got the lamebrain idea that we could fly in and out of Las Vegas and save money by staying at a hotel and leaving the car at no additional cost.

As is bound to happen, I woke up the morning of our Vegas trek with one of those serious sore throats. My immunity was shot, and someone had coughed in my face one too many times. I was getting pretty sick with a low-grade temperature and trying to control it by popping 400 mg of ibuprofen.

Covering my virtual reference hours on the trip sounded like a good idea at the time. My hours fell the next day 9 am to 11 am. Our flight didn't leave until 3:25 pm, and the hotel provided free Internet service. Brett College's commitment to satisfying the requirements for our virtual reference hours could be fulfilled on the sixth floor of a Las Vegas hotel, allowing unbroken 24/7 access to our students, even around Christmas.

The next morning I awoke at 7:15 am, showered, and munched on a tasty scrambled-egg croissant in the hotel's downstairs restaurant with my wife and two young daughters before packing up and being ready for the airport shuttle pick up at 1:30 pm. Getting connected to the hotel's Internet service on my office laptop worked on the second try. As I struggled with my cold and situated myself for monitoring the online service, my four-year-old Vicki came up to me and said, "Daddy, my ear is slow."

"What?" I replied. "What do you mean your ear is slow?"

Then, as only a four-year-old can do, she carefully picked up my ear thermometer, turned it on, and placed it in her ear. It soon beeped. She removed it from her ear, looked at the digital readout, and showed it to me. It displayed "Lo." Then with sarcastic confidence, she said, "See, I told you so."

My mind went fuzzy. I chuckled. It was now 9:07 am, and the ubiquitous single tone from my computer reminded me that my first patron was waiting to come on the screen. I ignored further distractions and plunged into my work, thinking, "Now, whose idea was this any way? Oh yeah, mine."

I clicked on the patron's identity, Nancy. Immediately next to her name displayed the small pulsating vertical line of my cursor, representing the only sense in the universe that I or one of the other twenty-three librarians monitoring at that moment would get her. Then, bingo! My screen evolved into Nancy's question. "APA FORMATTING" is all it said. We were chatting live. Without thinking, I cleared my throat, straightened up my back, and tried to forget about my fever while typing.

**Librarian:** Hi Nency, do you have a reference question?

*Oops, I'd typed too fast. First impression went out the door. Wasn't it Dale Carnegie in* How to Win Friends and Influence People *who said a person's name was the sweetest sound?*[3] *I attempted to redeem myself.*

**Librarian:** Sorry, Nancy.

*I waited. A few seconds passed and then.*

**Patron:** Putting this information in formatting

**Patron:** http://edu.nursinglink.com

*Hmm, not even a hint of an informal hi. Her words were like small table morsels swept off by an uncaring hand. But my library school training made my mind stick with a more forgiving (some might think naive) scenario. Perhaps she's in a hurry and distracted. Let's see; her query appears to be an APA issue, otherwise known as following the writing style found in the* Publication Manual of the American Psychological Association. *I quickly brought up another web browser, went to Google, typed "owl apa," and up came an APA-style OWL (Online Writing Lab) website. I copied the site's URL and then typed.*

**Librarian:** APA. OK, I might suggest you look at this website for APA formatting: http://owl.english.purdue.edu/owl/resource/560/01/.[4]

*I quickly followed the URL link she'd sent and noticed that it was a nursing website. I continued.*

**Librarian:** OK, I'm on the nursing webpage. Do you need to cite this page as a web source in APA style?

*Due to the lack of response from a patron, the virtual librarian occasionally misses the luxury of the interactive question negotiation phase that face-to-face reference interviews have. Lacking question negotiation, the so-called interview becomes part mystery game and part spontaneous intuition to get to the next step. I had to second-guess what the patron really needed. I felt that giving a little more information from the APA website might help.*

**Librarian:** On the site I gave you above, under "Reference List: Electronic Sources," it has the following example for webpages . . .

*I then simply copied and pasted a few lines from the webpage and sent then to Nancy, focusing on the essential parts for citing a webpage in a bibliography according to APA. There was still no response. The green dot next to her name had yet to turn red to indicate that she left the session. We were still live. What more could I do, except maybe give the full answer? Well, I wasn't doing anything else on the sixth floor of a Las Vegas hotel. So, I committed myself to go the extra mile.*

**Librarian:** Let me see if I can suggest a proper APA-style citation.

*Studying the nursing website, I noticed that it did not have an explicit author.*

**Librarian:** This site doesn't appear to have an author, so I'll use something that looks like a corporate author. Just a moment.

*She probably doesn't have a clue what a corporate author is nor care, but I wanted her to know that I was still working, and working hard, on her question.*

**Librarian:** How about this: NursingLink. (2007). Nurses are in demand. Retrieved December 22, 2007, from http://edu.nursinglink.com/.[5]

**Librarian:** And the words "Nurses are in demand" would be in italics.

*Still no response. I'd come to the end of my answer for this question. It seems that I get there sooner when in virtual mode than in other reference media. Nevertheless, at this threshold, I'm reminded of the most statistically significant phrases that can clinch a right answer.*

**Librarian:** Does that completely answer your question?

*I then added my own spin.*

**Librarian:** Is there anything else? Glad to help if so.

*I was now thinking that I would just end the session and move on when, suddenly, the silence of more than twenty minutes was broken.*

**Patron:** Yes. I need a site to help me put information in references form.

*Augh! I felt like Charlie Brown. Maybe her name was really Lucy. Hadn't she read what I sent? Maybe she was multitasking. This faceless, voiceless experience can be numbing. I waited. Less than three minutes passed and then the final straw came.*

**Patron:** Patron ended chat session.

*Her green dot turned red. Somehow I felt that was coming. She had typed an e-mail address at the beginning of her session. Assuming it was correct, I continued the conversation believing that she'd received the full transcript in her e-mail.*

**Librarian:** The site I gave you above gives APA style for reference lists and should work for you. If not, log back in and feel free to ask another librarian.

*I closed with the following prewritten script.*

**Librarian:** Thank you for using our "Ask a Librarian" service. If you need any further help, log back in for a new chat session. Good-bye.

*I set the resolution as answered and logged out of Nancy's session. I blinked my eyes, took a deep sigh, and hunched down in my chair. My instinctive four-year-old read my body language as the perfect time to show me her newest piece of word art.*

"Daddy, Daddy, here, read this," Vicki said as she plopped on my laptop keyboard a piece of hotel stationery with scribbles on it. I played along.

"Oh, what's this?" I pondered. "Hmm, let me see," as I read, "ipoud is pedo lam doi no do lap odilly Vicki," and paused before summarizing, "Ah, it sounds like another language."

Vicki, without missing a beat, said, "Yes, it's Spanish. It's directions for going to the potty."

"Wow, sweetie, that's, ah, cute," I responded as my laptop speaker announced another patron. "Sorry, honey, Dad's got to go." I immediately clicked on the patron's name and jumped right in. Her name was Sandy, and her question related to information on the child care industry.

**Librarian:** Hi Sandy, I'm reading your question.

*In just seven seconds, there was an answer.*

**Patron:** OK.

*Great, she responded! I quickly clicked on her library's information and found a couple of possible databases. Co-browsing was not possible, so I needed to look at resources that I could access from my library's databases back home at Brett College. I felt like Sandy might be a more active patron. I intended to get a lot of mileage out of her two letters, "OK," so I continued.*

**Librarian:** I'm on your library's website. I suggest that you start with College Explore Premier. I have access to it from my library. Let me try your topic, and let's see if we can find a few relevant articles for you. What is your assignment? Do you need scholarly articles, and how many?

**Patron:** Any articles will help. I'm doing research on the child care industry, and I need information on the market and the industry, the history, trends, competition, strengths, and weaknesses.

*Well, nothing like an easy question. Who cares if I'm in Vegas with a fever? I'm going for broke.*

**Librarian:** Oh, then we need to try a business industry database. One moment.

**Patron:** OK, thanks.

**Librarian:** I see your library (like mine) has XYZ/BusInform—one of the best on business and industry information. Let me see what I can find.

**Patron:** OK.

**Librarian:** I found that "Child care AND Day care centers" are subject headings, and I'm now trying to see if there are narrower subtopics getting at your question. One moment.

**Patron:** No problem. I appreciate the help.

**Librarian:** There is a subject area called "trends," and I brought up 26 articles.

*We were on a roll.*

**Patron:** OK.

**Patron:** Where can I find it?

*I could see by my search results that most of the articles were not relevant to her topic.*

**Librarian:** Hmm, not good. They are very dated (1996 and older). Let me try a different angle to get more of what you need. Just a moment.

**Patron:** OK.

**Librarian:** While I'm searching, why don't you go to your library's database and on the left-hand side choose XYZ/BusInform, type in "Child care AND Day care centers" and choose "subject." I retrieved 348 entries.

**Patron:** Nice.

**Librarian:** Again, most of these are not as relevant as I thought. Let's try something more productive. In "Databases" on your library site, choose "Business" next to "Select Subject."

**Patron:** OK, I did that.

**Librarian:** The third database is Industry Observe Online, which includes "market research reports on 14 industry sectors in 50 global markets."

**Patron:** OK.

**Librarian:** Also, the last database listed is Global Horizon, which "generates reports of US global competitors."

**Patron:** OK will search both databases.

*We soon hit pay dirt within what some in the profession call the "rhythm of chat," the point when the librarian and patron form a kind of rhythmic communication. Messages dance between computer screens. Magic happens.*

**Librarian:** The three major child care companies are Children's Wonderland, Inc., La Petite Academy, Inc., and New Horizon Kids Quest, Inc.

**Patron:** Yes thank you.

**Patron:** I will look up these companies and get information from them.

We continued like this for another twenty minutes, breaking all the rules on normal chat reference duration. In the end, she had a rich source of marketing data, and I was dead tired.

The dance came to an end as our virtual music stopped. I said bye to my partner and closed out the session. My two-hour session was now up.

My wife had gone out for Chinese bowls of hot noodles, rice, meat, and soft drinks. I closed up my laptop when Vicki piped up.

"I want to say the prayer," she demanded.

"OK, honey, you can say grace," I said, appeasing her request.

As the four of us grabbed one another's hands in a circle, Vicki closed her eyes and began.

"Thank you for the food. Thank you for the sky. Thank you for the world. Thank you for the people. And thank you for the letter of the day," followed by a few giggles and "Amen."

I wondered if Sesame Street knew how eloquently its "letter of the day" had been prayed over that day. I began to slump a little, eating rice and meat as my cold demanded rest. The television was turned on. A small group of voices softly filled our room on the sixth floor of our Las Vegas hotel with "Away in a manger, no crib for his bed . . . "

My feverish mind rested within the lullaby's magic as I reflected on the two virtual patrons and the added context of my daughter's conversations. How infrequently we allow small children to lead us toward appropriate moments of peace on Earth and goodwill toward humankind. Merry Christmas, Las Vegas.

## REFLECTIONS

### Knowledge

- Make a list of three similarities and three differences between the first chat patron and the second.
- As the librarian was trying to monitor chat reference, how many times was he interrupted and by whom?
- What one thing did the librarian do on the first chat that might make Dale Carnegie cringe?

### Comprehension

- Go to an AskNow chat reference site (your university or local public library should have one) or go to http://liswiki.org/wiki/Chat_ reference_libraries. Make up a question, such as how to cite one of the

resources in this book (e.g., APA, MLA, or Chicago style) or something else. A copy of your transcript should be sent to your e-mail.
- Go to the blog for this book at http://referenceinterview.wordpress.com/, click the part for this chapter (Scenario 4—Virtual in Vegas), and post a brief discussion of your chat experience (conducted in the previous bullet).
- Reread the reference interview with the second chat patron. Why did the librarian change from the first suggested database (College Explore Premier) to the second one (XYZ/BusInform)?
- Describe what you think the *rhythm of chat* is and why it is important.

## Application

- Looking at both chats from this scenario, what one or two things would you do differently as the chat librarian?
- What is the main idea of this scenario, and why is it important?
- Make up one or more ways to measure chat experiences (e.g., length of session in time; difficulty of question; number of keystrokes by patron, librarian, and both; subject matter—see chapter 16 for more ideas). Which classifications would the first chat fall into? The second?

## Analysis

- Describe two differences and two similarities between these chat reference interviews.
- What was the turning point (tipping point) of the interview in the first chat? The second chat?
- How would you handle a chat patron like the first one, who seemed to be not responding in a timely manner? Log off earlier? Refer the chat patron to another librarian?

## Synthesis

- Compose a song or poem about this reference chat scenario.
- Invent a different way that both these reference questions could be answered by a service that has yet to be created.
- If you could change what chat interface looks like to the patrons before they begin to ask their questions, based on these two interactions, what notice or notices would you post on their end for them to read that might make the interview go more smoothly?

## Evaluation

- Let's say that both these chat patrons were using a public library chat service somewhere in the United States and did not have access to proprietary databases. How would you still answer their questions? (Clue: Google Scholar)
- Justify the kinds of preferred skills that a patron (e.g., K–12 student, public library user, college student, adult learner) would need to conduct a successful chat reference interview with a librarian.
- Judge and write about whether the librarian did any information literacy during both these reference interviews. What could he do to improve this, if anything?

## NOTES

Originally published in *Reference Librarian* in 2008: Dave Harmeyer, "Virtual in Vegas," *Reference Librarian* 49, no. 2 (2008): 171–77.

1. Dave Harmeyer, "Online Virtual Chat Library Reference Service: A Quantitative and Qualitative Analysis [PhD diss., Pepperdine University, 2007]," *Dissertation Abstracts International*, 68/10; one of two results chapters is reproduced in chapter 16, "A Conceptual Model for Online Chat Reference Answer Accuracy."

2. Anthony S. Chow and Rebecca A. Croxton, "A Usability Evaluation of Academic Virtual Reference Services," *College and Research Libraries*, http://crl.acrl.org/content/early/2013/02/06/crl13-408.full.pdf.

3. Dale Carnegie, *How to Win Friends and Influence People* (New York: Simon & Schuster, 1981), 79.

4. "The Online Writing Lab (OWL) at Purdue University," http://owl.english.purdue.edu/owl/.

5. "Nurses Are in Demand," *NursingLink* (2007), http://edu.nursinglink.com/.

*Chapter Seven*

# Scenario 5

*An Unlikely Answer under a Window of Stained Glass*

I'd guess that most reference professionals, if given the choice, would say that they are more a generalist than a specialist, even if they shepherded a *special* collection or a *special* library, such as law, business, music, or theology. This generalist tendency makes us crazy about learning almost anything. I don't know if you've ever been to a museum with someone who enjoyed reading ALL the artifact signage, but apart from being somewhat annoying, this tells me that one has the gift of being a generalist, knowing a little something about a lot. I think generalists make good reference librarians because not only can they handle a wide spectrum of queries, but for those about which they have little idea, their generalist spirit helps them genuinely be engaged in the topic and often serendipitously find the answer.[1] In the following scenario, the librarian highlights what I mean about the generalist spirit, question engagement, and a spark of serendipitous insight.

## THE SCENARIO

Everyone instinctively looks straight up when entering the rotunda at Brett College's library. At the top of a three-story, cone-shaped ceiling is a massive stained-glass window. The commissioned oval-shaped mosaic of epoxy glass artistically displays the four cornerstones of the 107-year-old faith-based institution: God, Service, Scholarship, and Community. The bottom-right quadrant depicts an open book symbolizing the third stone: Scholarship. Small white globes passing through the structure's permeable outer rim illustrate knowledge as it filters in and out of the world.

It was three minutes before 10 am, and I was comfortably on time for a weekly meeting as the library representative for the college's Research and Development Council. The group had been charged by the board to experiment with new ways to increase our online programs, and I was eager to share a few trends in the field of librarianship. As I stepped from outside the library into the quiet, high-ceiling rotunda, my head turned up out of habit. My mortal eyes fell on the angelic glow of the large, colorful stained-glass image. This time, my wits compelled me to reflect for a moment on the bottom-right quadrant, Scholarship. However, I was just about to find myself much later to my meeting than what the momentary musings that an art object would allow.

"Dave, we need your help," someone cried in a loud whisper.

My outstretched neck lowered and turned slightly left toward the library's circulation desk and the voice that had cut short my pleasurable glance above.

"Oh, Diane. Hi. Ah, what's up?" I asked in earnest. Diane was the library's head circulation coordinator, and for several years, this responsible, cheerful Brett College graduate had loved supervising students and meeting the needs of each library user.

"You know, Dave, it's too early for a librarian at the reference desk, and Marilyn Abbot has me stumped on what we thought would be a simple find. Can you help her out?"

I smiled at Diane and said, "Umm, sure," as my eyes met Marilyn's hopeful face.

Dr. Marilyn Abbot was a popular, well-published faculty member at Brett, teaching classes in physical education and chairing its growing department. She had served with me on a program review committee a few years back, where I came to respect her scholarly pursuits.

"Good to see you again, Dave. I'm trying to find a certain questionnaire used frequently in the literature to measure a person's spirituality. It's called the Spiritual Perspective Scale. I've come across four or five questions from it, but I need the whole thing. Can you help?"

"Sure," I said, looking for a quick Indiana Jones way to find the questionnaire and still get to my meeting in reasonable time. Right in front of us was one of the library's dedicated book catalog monitors, so I merely typed in the title of the questionnaire to see if any books might contain the survey. One item appeared on the screen, but it was a false hit, a book on human nature and spiritual perspectives.

"No good there. Let's try something else," I suggested.

Normally these stand-alone terminals connect people to only the library's online catalog. But I knew a quick work-around, and in a few seconds, we were on the library's website with our 120 databases. I was thinking, "I know right where to go."

"OK, have you tried the survey database called SaDLI? It stands for Survey Database with Lots of Instruments. It indexes hundreds of question-naire instruments found in journal articles and even includes information on purchasing the surveys themselves."

"Yeah, Dave, I've tried SaDLI. I figured that the oldest articles might have the original questionnaire. But the articles were in the 1980s and outside the library's full-text databases. Articles that had the questionnaire in the library's paper journals had only a few of the questions. I'm looking for all ten."

I quickly confirmed Marilyn's findings by bringing up the SaDLI data-base and entered the words "Spiritual Perspective Scale." I typed it within quotation marks so that the search would retrieve the three words as a bounded phrase, a technique that provides better-quality results. The default setting on the search was by relevance, which generally puts articles contain-ing the most number of phrases or words sought at the top of the list. Nine items came up, with the oldest being 1987. Marilyn was right; most of the older articles were outside our digital holdings, and I took her word that our paper copies didn't have the full questionnaire.

"I have a lamebrain idea. Let's try Google Scholar and see if someone's put the whole scale up on the free Internet," I suggested.

I typed in "scholar.google.com" and copy and pasted "Spiritual Perspec-tive Scale" in its search engine box. In sum, 303 items came up. All included the three-word phrase, but as I clicked on the first dozen links, none brought up anything in full text, let alone the full questionnaire. We did get plenty of publishers' websites, third-party pay-per-views, expanded abstracts of the article, and even small excerpts from parts of whole articles. But there was nothing useful.

At this moment, I took a slow, purposeful glance up at that stained-glass window. The late-morning sun seemed to shine through it in an odd and mystical way. Time seemed to stop. I drew a long, bottomless breath and released a sigh. I felt I was in slow motion. There was calm. Then there came a spark of inspiration, straight out of the bottom right quadrant of Scholar-ship. My mind returned to the situation at hand, and I said, "You know, Marilyn, I've been reviewing the front matter of dissertations lately. Doctoral students provide an uncanny amount of detail about their dissertation pro-cess, including the actual survey instruments used in their data finding and analysis. I wonder if our access to the full text of dissertations might help you out here." While I suggested this, Marilyn's eyes got as big as the impassive evocative globes in the window.

I clicked back to our database page and brought up the vendor's index that provided access to the full text of doctoral dissertations and master's theses. I pasted the three-word phrase that we'd come to expect great results from into the search engine box but so far got nothing helpful . . . until now.

"Look at that," I said. "Thirty dissertations came up! If I'm right, at least some of these should have all ten questions from the questionnaire." I changed the order of sort from "Relevance" to "Publication date (most recent)" to get the most up-to-date scale so that we could determine if there were any revisions to it. We looked at the first two dissertations, but neither had the full scale. I clicked on the title link of the third entry, "The Function of Spirituality, Social Interest, Life Satisfaction, and Materialism in Moderating Death Anxiety in College Students."[2] In bold yellow highlight, our three-letter phrase glowed near the beginning of the abstract in a promising way.

"Hmm, this looks good. The author is clearly stating that the spiritual scale was used along with a few other instruments. Let's open up the full text and see what's listed in her appendices," I said as I moved my cursor to click on the full-text link.

It was a 126-page dissertation. The full digital copy was on the screen in eight seconds. I carefully scrolled down to the table of contents and listed as Appendix E was "Questionnaire Packet," page 91.

I impatiently scrolled to page 91, and soon, after a few other surveys passed by, on page 97 up flashed the ten questions over a two-page layout. I copied the two pages of questions and pasted them to a separate document.

"Now, let's see how the instrument was cited," I said as I moved the screen back to the table of contents.

I continued, "There's little detail listed under 'Chapter III: Methods,' where surveys would normally be mentioned. So let's do a search for the phrase 'Spiritual Perspective Scale.'" On the second occurrence in the manuscript, the doctoral student had properly cited the instrument as coming from Reed in 1986, and then we looked up the full citation in the bibliography.[3]

"Wow! Great, Dave!" she gasped. "I would never have thought of looking at the end of a dissertation to get this questionnaire. Umm, could you back up a little and show me how you did that again?"

"Sure," I said enthusiastically, as I began to review. "First, you want to confirm the name of the scale by checking its title in the SaDLI index."

"Right," interrupted Marilyn. "Then I'd try to locate the articles that are cited in SaDLI. You might get lucky and find that the library actually has the full text and, possibly, the instrument in one of those articles."

"You got it," I confirmed. "And if you plan to use that instrument in one of your studies, you can purchase copies from a vendor, if listed, in SaDLI, or you can get permission directly from the author. That's what the 'Anxiety in College Students' doctoral student did. If you'll notice, just before the questionnaire, there's a digitized request form from the author, Pamela G. Reed," I said as I moved the screen back to the e-mail correspondence and form I'd seen earlier. "You can use the student's examples as a model for your own request."

I glanced over at Marilyn and continued, "Now, if you can't find the full instrument from what you get in the SaDLI index, either go to the free Internet using Google Scholar because it's possible that the entire thing may be posted, or try the dissertations and theses database by typing in the title of the questionnaire, just as I did."

"I think I've got it now, Dave. Good work. Sorry, I've got to go. Can you just send what you have to my e-mail?" she asked as she moved away from the catalog screen and hurried out the front doors.

"Sure," I called after her as I pushed the last button, sending the document to her campus e-mail.

I returned the screen to its original online catalog interface and waved a quick good-bye to the circulation coordinator as I got up.

"Thanks, Dave. That's one for the books!" said Diane.

Hurrying through the stately rotunda, I was now twenty-three minutes late to my meeting, yet I still found a few moments to glance up into that colorful friend above.

"Thanks for the inspiration," I whispered to the pensive pieces of glass and dashed on out.

## REFLECTIONS

### Knowledge

- Make a sequential list (first, second, third, etc.) of the main points in this reference transaction.
- What is the name of the survey/instrument database that the librarian first went to, and why is this important?
- Go to Google Scholar (http://scholar.google.com/), conduct a search of "Spiritual Perspective Scale" (with quotation marks, perspective is singular), and compare your results to those mentioned in the scenario. Then try searching in Google with the same phrase. This method was not mentioned in the scenario . . . see why!

### Comprehension

- What is the main idea of this scenario? Hint: It is not using Google Scholar to find everything!
- Cut out or draw a picture to illustrate a particular event in this scenario.
- Name three techniques that the librarian performed that could be defined as information literacy instruction. Remember: Information literacy is a set of abilities requiring individuals to recognize when information is

needed and to have the ability to locate, evaluate, and effectively use the needed information. [4]

## Application

- Construct up to six categories of reference interview question types and put this scenario's question into one of them. Hint: See chapter 16, paragraph 2 in the section titled Coding Procedures (p. 136).
- What factors would you have changed in this scenario if such a faculty member interrupted you as you were making your way to a meeting?
- Make a diorama to illustrate an important event in this scenario.

## Analysis

- List at least three dead ends encountered during this reference transaction (i.e., did not find anything useful).
- Go to the blog for this book at http://referenceinterview.wordpress.com/, click on the part for this chapter (Scenario 5—An Unlikely Answer under a Window of Stained Glass), and in your own words post a brief comment on where you think the tipping point (turning point) occurred in this scenario.
- Identify four characteristics of the librarian before he entered the library. Hint: He was willing to answer questions when not expected.

## Synthesis

- What additional training would you recommend for Diane and her circulation staff so that they can effectively meet the need of such questions by faculty members such as Dr. Marilyn Abbot? Alternatively, discuss justifications why such a question should be answered by only a professional librarian.
- Devise your own way to deal with the question from this scenario that is different from what the librarian did.
- Act out this scenario with another individual, then reverse the roles and discuss how you felt.

## Evaluation

- Create two sides of a debate: first, that circulation staff should be trained to answer reference questions; second, that they should not be trained to do so. Perform the debate in front of a class.

- Prepare a list of criteria to judge a reference interview. Hint: See Reference and User Services Association's "Guidelines for Behavioral Performance of Reference and Information Services" at http://www.ala.org/rusa/resources/guidelines/guidelinesbehavioral.
- Suppose that a week later, Dr. Abbot and this librarian meet again in a hallway. Predict what they might say about what Dr. Abbot remembers from their last time together. With this as an example of a reference interview with a faculty member, how much should librarians expect faculty to recall from such a conversation?

## NOTES

Originally published in *Reference Librarian* in 2009: Dave Harmeyer, "An Unlikely Answer under a Window of Stained Glass," *Reference Librarian* 50, no. 2 (2009): 208–11.

1. This is not to say that a question is not to be referred to a reference specialist when appropriate. Chapter 16 provides statistical support that questions unanswered within a span of time, at least in the chat environment, should be passed on sooner rather than later or risk lower answer accuracy.

2. Lisa VanderVeer, "The Function of Spirituality, Social Interest, Life Satisfaction, and Materialism in Moderating Death Anxiety in College Students [PhD diss., Adler School of Professional Psychology, 2009]," *Dissertation Abstracts International* 73/07E.

3. Pamela G. Reed, "Developmental Resources and Depression in the Elderly: A Longitudinal Study," *Nursing* 35 no. 6 (1986): 368–74.

4. Association of College and Research Libraries, "Information Literacy Competency Standards for Higher Education," January 18, 2000, http://www.ala.org/acrl/standards/informationliteracycompetency.

*Chapter Eight*

# Scenario 6

*Earthquake Reference*

Natural disasters that happen around the world make compelling, dramatic news stories—that is, as long as they're not in our own backyard! Nevertheless, when they do occur near our loved ones, coworkers, and us, the threat to life is real, and we react with unpredictable levels of fear, whereas a few of us respond with calm control. At some point, after the danger appears over, there's a universal behavior for seeking current, accurate information about what just happened. What an honorable assignment that would be for a quick-thinking reference librarian with the right tools. This next scenario attempts to portray just such a situation, illustrating how a reference transaction is particularly useful during a natural disaster for the quick-thinking reference librarian.

### THE SCENARIO

It was late morning near the end of our summer programming at Richardson Public Library in the city of Richardson, California, thirty miles east of Los Angeles, when things at the library got a little shaken up. I was in one of the library's 12- by 10-foot study rooms with Mark Powell, the new head of collection development. We were deep in conversation. Our choice to move out of our cluttered offices afforded the undistracted attention that we needed to problem-solve one of our library's ever-present tribulations: lack of shelf space.

"So, I guess we'll see what the other librarians think about putting some of our annual budget toward an off-site repository," I summarized. "Yeah," continued Mark, "by using checkout data, we should be able to mark every book not borrowed in the past five years with a colored sticker. Then librarians can decide if those books go off-site or not. Any book could be retrieved in a twenty-four-hour turnaround. That should take us from our current 95 percent full shelves to close to 50 percent."

I added, "Then every year a new batch of older books not checked out would automatically be removed to the remote site, making room for newer acquisitions."

Mark suggested, "Our collections would, in practice, function as a kind of living organism—something like Ranganathan's fifth rule of librarianship."[1]

I was about to counter with another observation when, with no warning, somewhere originating deep below the building's foundation came a sudden, hard, sharp jerk that moved our room a few inches, immediately followed by a sickening rolling feeling. It was as if a gigantic dump truck had just driven by our small room. Our hearts accelerated and adrenaline surged into our once relaxed bodies. It was unreal.

Time seemed to slow down, even stop. Our lives were measured in microseconds as we lurched for the doorknob just a few feet away. Our bodies moved instinctively to prevent almost certain entombment inside the study room. Mark's right hand reached the doorknob first and quickly turned our potential entrapment into freedom. The door swung open a few feet to reveal more of the surreal moment: the once stately walls and high ceiling were flexing grotesquely as if they were made out of rubber. An uncanny squeaking noise filled our ears as the building's stress limits became tested. All was in motion.

A calmer mind would have reminded me what Diane, my five-year-old, had demonstrated in our living room only a few weeks ago. Her kindergarten class had participated in a statewide earthquake drill. I could hear her precocious voice state, "Drop, cover, and hold, Daddy. That's what we're supposed to do in an earthquake."

But we didn't. The large, double-paned window that acted as the wall to the left of the door thankfully remained intact as Mark and I stood gawking at the jerking episode around us. It felt like minutes, but it probably wasn't much more than a few seconds. Happily for us, it soon stopped.

From our vantage point in the center of the library's main floor, we watched as scores of patrons in the building began to panic and some started running. Mark took charge as we emerged from the room.

"Everyone!" he shouted in a strong, forceful voice. "Stay calm! Don't run. Walk to the nearest exit!" Eventually, most of the anxious-faced library users slowed down and walked, in an eerie silence, to the main exit and outside to safety.

The library had upper and lower floors of book stacks. Mark instinctively moved toward the staircase door. He shouted back at me, "You take the top floor, and I'll check the bottom."

I responded, "Sure, be careful," as I followed behind and started up the staircase. By the time I'd reached the top floor, I realized that the building's alarm system had been triggered and was now throbbing relentlessly in my ears, accompanied by the system's strobe lights pulsating on random walls.

The noise and brightness added to the freaky chaos as I quickly checked down what used to be quiet rows of common shelving. Luckily, I didn't find anyone trapped under the few piles of books that had fallen to the floor. The top floor was all clear, and I exited back to the main floor.

Knowing that earthquakes are followed by aftershocks, I was eager to get outside the structure and quickly away from danger. However, as I reached the library's lobby, I remembered that my laptop was still in my office. Without considering the danger, I turned around and went back into the belly of the library, coping with the constant beep-beep-beep and flashing lights of the building's alarm system. In a few moments, I entered my windowless office, quickly unplugged the electrical cord and external mouse from my computer, tucked the unit under my arm, and hurried back toward the exit. I was relieved when I finally pushed open one of the glass front doors, breathing the fresh air and welcoming the summer sunlight, only then realizing the risk I'd taken.

At a safe distance from the library's south-facing entrance stood a group of chest-high black-metal tables that patrons used for eating food from the vending machines. On one of them, I opened up my laptop and unintentionally soon found myself playing the role of a kind of command center reference librarian—have battery-operated laptop, will travel.

A half-dozen people who had exited the library and other buildings nearby were recovering from the quake's nerve-wracking effects. They began to collect their thoughts and mill about. Most were now anxious for news on the ordeal. A man in a polo shirt with long dark hair who was holding a large group of folders and books under his arm came over to my table and asked, "Ah, excuse me, but aren't you one of the reference librarians?"

I responded, "Sure am. What's your name?"

"Frank. Say, have you found out anything about where that quake was centered?"

"Well, Frank, that's certainly the question of the moment. Let's see if we can find out," I answered as I brought up a browser on my screen.

Fortunately, the earthquake had not affected the library's wi-fi connection or the city's wireless network. I was soon on a search screen and typing "Southern California earthquake." A bunch of website links came up relating to past quakes but not the one that happened fifteen minutes ago.

"Hmm, nothing there . . . "

I wasn't sure where to go for this one. Then, I thought, if I wanted the most up-to-date information on something that had just happened, I'd turn on a radio news station.

I continued, "Let's try one of our local radio news stations' websites."

In the search engine, I typed KFWB, and the first link that came up was Hollywood's "KFWB NEWS 980—Homepage." Under this was a list of sublinks, including one that said "Quake Center." I clicked on it, and the screen that came up was a chart of data from recent earthquakes all over the world listed on individual horizontal lines. Sure enough, the top entry was a quake that occurred today at 11:52 am, two miles southwest of Chino Hills, California, with a magnitude of 5.4. Bingo!

"Wow, that's amazing. Hey folks, come over here and look at this." Soon there were five more people looking on. I think I'd just become the most popular librarian in Richardson.

In the group, one young woman with a red and black *I Love NY* T-shirt and denim jeans asked, "5.4—is that big? I'm from the Bronx, and this was my first big earthquake. How far did the quake hit from here?" she asked.

I kept my current browser open to the news station and opened a new browser. Here I brought up a map/direction website and typed the address for Richardson Public Library as the starting point and Chino Hills as the destination. I soon found out that the general driving distance by roads from the library to the city of Chino Hills was 18.5 miles southeast of here (good enough for us). I added two more miles for measure and answered, "Well, that makes it about 20 miles southeast of here."

It was now a little after 12:30 pm, forty minutes after the quake. I wondered if there were any live audio or video feeds of information. We were in luck. As I returned to the news station's website, there was something called "Earthquake Update." A news helicopter had flown over the epicenter, and a video report was on the webpage. I clicked on the link, and soon we were all watching a slightly pixeled image from the air, looking down on a flat terrain with buildings and small hills to the left. The image slightly bobbed as the announcer gave out his location and mentioned what we all saw on my laptop screen: "There appears to be a cloud of light dust rising from the general area. I can't quite make it out, but my guess is it was due to the earthquake. That's it for now; this is news chopper man Jim Donovan with KFWB signing off at 12:15." My guess is that the newscaster was already in the air broadcasting about a freeway mishap nearby when he got wind of the earthquake and changed his settings to Chino Hills.

Things had changed around us as well. Those six folks that initially came by had now grown into a small crowd. "That was awesome," said an older woman with what looked like her granddaughter. Then several voices spoke up at the same time, "Hey, can you find out if anyone got hurt in the area. Are my coworkers OK? When can we go back into the library?"

"Just a second, everyone; the city police department has a command center, and I'm sure it's been activated. Someone has probably posted a message on a web link off the city's main web page. Let me check."

Sure enough, as I moved my screen's location to the City of Richardson's front page, there under "News and Features" was a link to the Richardson Emergency Command Center's blog and an update on the earthquake. With a time stamp of 12:21 pm, the statement read,

> A magnitude 5.4 earthquake centering near Chino Hills, CA shook the city of Richardson at 11:52 a.m. today. All employees and people in the vicinity are to evacuate all buildings and maintain a safe distance from buildings and power lines.
>
> The city's fire and police departments are conducting building-to-building sweeps to access any personnel injuries and building damage. Please remain out of buildings until cleared by an officer. Thank you for your cooperation.
> RICHARDSON EMERGENCY COMMAND CENTER TEAM

"Hey, Dave, how's it going?" It was Mark, and he was a little out of breath.

I updated Mark by sharing, "Everything seems to be fine. I think everyone got out of the library with no problems, and there's been a message posted saying to stay out of buildings until an officer gives us the all-clear."

Mark added, "Yeah, I found that out, too. I tried calling the dispatch on my cell, but the connection was down, so I ran over to their offices on the next block. On the way, I met Officer Thomas, who was just coming out of the Ahmanson Building. They found some railing damage on the second floor, and so they weren't letting folks back in there just yet. He said he'd send someone over to the library soon."

"Great," I responded. I noticed that the small crowd started to break up and was waiting around until it could get back into the library.

"I think this will go down as one of the weirdest reference interviews I've ever had," I shared.

"How's that?" asked Mark.

"It's the only time that my reference question turned out to be the very event I'd just lived through," I reflected.

"All in a day's work, my friend!" Mark said, "All in a day's work."

## REFLECTIONS

### Knowledge

- See if you can make a timeline of events based on the information in this scenario.
- Why did the librarian go back into the library just to retrieve his laptop?

- Describe what the librarian found on the website of KFWB.

## Comprehension

- Explain why the librarian did not instruct anyone in information literacy during this reference transaction.
- Discuss additional patrons who likely benefited from the reference interview. Hint: People on cell phones talking to loved ones and coworkers.
- Make a cartoon strip showing the sequence of events.

## Application

- What other disasters (in any location) might a librarian realistically find herself or himself in that could result in a similar service to a community?
- What other resources could the librarian have used to gain additional information for the crowd?
- Go to the blog for this book at http://referenceinterview.wordpress.com/, click the part for this chapter (Scenario 6—Earthquake Reference), and post a set of librarian instructions for disaster reference—during and after—that can help needs of patrons.

## Analysis

- What was the underlying theme of this reference transaction?
- List three problems that could have happened in this reference interview that would have not made it successful.
- This transaction/interview had at least one tipping point (turning point). What was it?

## Synthesis

- Invent an information kiosk placed outside the city library that could dispense similar information illustrated in this reference interview. Hints: Touch screen? Pay or free? Voice activated? Wireless connection? Connected to 911? What does it look like?
- Propose a script for a television show, play, puppet show, role-play, song, or pantomime about this scenario.
- Describe what would happen next in this scenario if there were an aftershock stronger than a 5.4 magnitude!

## Evaluation

- Judge the value of this reference interview by listing three public good services that the librarian provided.
- Pretend that you are the librarian, and defend your position about returning into the library to retrieve you laptop.
- Based on this scenario, what additions or clarifications would you recommend to the library policies regarding what to do in a natural disaster, such as an earthquake, tornado, fire, or flood?

## NOTES

Originally published in *Reference Librarian* in 2009: Dave Harmeyer, "Earthquake Reference," *Reference Librarian* 50, no. 3 (2009): 297–301.

1. Shiyali Ramamrita Ranganathan, *The Five Laws of Library Science* (New York: Asia, 1963), 382.

*Chapter Nine*

# Scenario 7

*Helping Publish, Not Perish*

One area lacking between the reference professional and the academy is useful service through the faculty to the student as well as to the faculty member directly. Reference personnel focus so much on students that there is a service gap with the very ones who, according to the research, can have as great or greater impact meeting student learning outcomes for information literacy than librarians—that being teaching faculty.[1] On a related note, more can also be done between faculty's scholarship agendas and reference services to support those agendas. One example would be teaching faculty how to create saved searches on their research topics that run automatically when databases are updated. In addition to meeting the obvious bibliographic needs of the scholar/teacher, there are other services that reference personnel can provide. Another example would be to teach techniques for discovering peer-reviewed publications to which faculty can submit their manuscripts. The following scenario aligns a librarian in a place of favor with a faculty member who is looking for promising journals to publish in.

## THE SCENARIO

It was the third annual doctoral luncheon of Brett College's 110-year history. The atmosphere was celebratory and regal with a handful of professors from each of the seven doctoral programs. A large, circular Arthurian-like table graced the center of a large room, christened with white linens and filled with the college's best silver and other tableware. Smells of chicken cordon bleu, asparagus tips, and garlic-mashed potatoes filled the air as published scholars found their seats by calligraphy-scripted name cards and then sipped large goblets of raspberry iced tea. Dr. Ruth Gobelt, chair of the doctoral council's scholarship committee, finished off her introductory remarks by proposing,

> Now, as has become our custom, let's go around the table and share your name and a little about your current research. I know it's hard to believe, but our lives are so busy these days we hardly know one another or what we're doing. So, let's start with you, Devin.

What followed was a scholarly parade of professors who, in their respective fields of study, shared research agendas that would make any regional accreditation team take notice. There was a School of Education professor who, from the perspective of moral imagination, passionately summarized her studies on high-achieving, economically disadvantaged students. A faculty member from the doctor of physical therapy program described his study on patient satisfaction with orthotics designed to reduce the chronic pain of plantar fasciitis. A team from both the School of Theology and the School of Psychology doctoral faculty updated the group on their $300,000 grant to study Pentecostals who place themselves in harm's way for the sake of justice movements.

Sitting among these inspiring researchers were a few of Brett College's faculty librarians. Their presence highlighted the fact that librarians served the doctoral needs of their assigned schools and programs. Approximately two-thirds of the way into the introductions, our library's associate dean, Dr. Stewart Rutherford, added to the experience,

> And I'm Stu Rutherford, associate dean of the library and the library representative on the doctoral council. In addition to my most recent research on quantitative and qualitative assessment of chat reference, with two articles and a book chapter pending, I wanted to mention that the library liaison to your department is available to help not only with your students' dissertation literature review needs but also with your own personal research requests. One area I think we may all struggle in is finding appropriate peer-reviewed journals for our manuscript submissions. Please contact your department's librarian to help with this and other reference needs. On behalf of the library and its faculty and staff, we look forward to helping you with significant growth in all of Brett College's current and future doctoral programs.

The luncheon continued with the rest of the introductions while members finished off servings of strawberry cheesecake and coffee. Dr. Gobelt concluded the event with the formal announcement of the college's five $10,000 grant awardees and officially adjourned the luncheon.

As faculty began to disperse and mingle, some congratulating an award winner, others probing for more information on a researcher's work, a tall, thin man looking somewhat distraught came up and shook my hand before expressing his thoughts in a voice of concern, "Hi Dave. Nice show, wasn't it? By the way, I'm in a rather tight spot right now and wondered if you might have a few moments to help me out."

It was Dr. Stanley Schoenleber, chair of the graduate department in the School of Business.

"You're right Stan, yes quite a show. You look anxious. What's up?" I responded.

"Well, it's my extended contract portfolio. I'm under a deadline to get an article submitted, but I'm having trouble finding a publisher. Your associate dean just mentioned something about how you could help in that area. Is that right?" he asked with a slightly forced smile.

"Certainly! I'm more than happy to help out." I pulled out my smartphone and consulted its calendar. "Let's see, hmmm. I don't have anything for the next hour or so. How about we meet over in the rose garden and try to solve your dilemma? We'd be less distracted," I suggested.

"Great! I have a few notes I'd like to pick up in my office. I'll see you there in ten minutes," Stan said as he started off in the direction of his office.

"And I'll bring my laptop," I responded, but he was out of hearing range.

In a few moments, we rendezvoused at the campus's decades-old rose garden. Some of the college community had fashioned it to be a secret garden because of its limited access via a few hidden passages, one so narrow that the script "The Gap" was embellished on its wall. The garden was within a rectangular courtyard surrounded by a series of in-facing undergraduate offices for the Department of English and Communication, adding to its medieval English Renaissance ambiance.

We began the reference interview sitting on one of the garden's rustic wooden benches. Overarched above us was a trellis of red, white, rose, and pink roses in full bloom. Whiffs of intoxicating fragrances from the flowers only invigorated our determination for the work ahead.

Sitting with my laptop open and connected to Brett's campuswide network, I asked Stan, "So tell me a little more about your article."

"Well, there are two," he began in earnest. "One deals with service learning and the other with transfer students. I'm kind of embarrassed, Dave. You'd think I'd know of journals to submit my manuscripts to, but I'm new to these fields of study, and, frankly, I don't know what journals may cover these areas."

"No problem. Let me suggest that, in the end, I hope that we find a couple of journals that will work in both subject areas. Then we'll locate their websites to get directions for author submissions. Also, in your cover letter, it wouldn't hurt to mention any recent articles they've published that are similar to yours. I'll cover that as well."

"Yeah, I've used that technique a couple of times in previous manuscripts, and it seems to help."

I continued, "For fun, let's just see if the term 'service learning' is in the title of a journal we own. I'm on our library's website and here's the link to all the full-text journal titles that we subscribe to. I'm typing 'service learning' inside double quotation marks, so the search is made as a phrase, keeping the two words together."

What displayed on my screen surprised both of us.

Stan's eyes grew big as he exclaimed, "Well, would you look at that! There's a journal called *Michigan Journal of Community Service Learning.*"

"OK, now let's hop on over to the journal's webpage," I said as I brought up another browser and typed *Michigan Journal of Community Service Learning* into a Google search. In moments, I was reading Stan the following: "'Since 1994, the *Michigan Journal of Community Service Learning* has been the premiere national, peer-reviewed journal publishing articles written by faculty and service-learning educators on research, theory, pedagogy, and other issues related to academic, curriculum-based, service learning in higher education.' How's that?"

"Dave, you blow me away! Can you send me that URL?"

"Sure. And here's the link to their submission guidelines," I added.

Stan changed his demeanor, "But how do we know they're telling the truth? It almost sounds too good to be true."

"Fair question. Let me see. OK, how about this? The library subscribes to a database that includes all paper and electronic journals published, including this one. Each record gives the number of libraries that own this title. That should give you a sense of how widely read this publication really is."

In a few minutes, my screen projected the record of this journal as well as the number of libraries that held it. The total was 246.

I stated, "Hmm, I'd suggest 246 is a pretty good number, considering the subject matter."

"Good point," Stan reflected. "But how can I find others?"

"That's an easy one. Notice in this record that the term 'service learning' is a *descriptor*. That's library talk for *subject heading*. We can do another search with this as a *subject heading* and then limit by journals as a medium."

The results of our search were revealing. Ninety-nine records designated as serials came up, and when I sorted by the number of libraries owning each title, the first one was the Michigan one.

"Again, Dave, it's amazing that we have that kind of information at our fingertips. And I can see that the next promising journal is something called *Journal of Public Affairs.*"

"Yes, that's true. And did you notice that you'd likely never have found that title had you not searched for it by the *subject heading* since neither the word 'service' nor 'learning' was in its title. Also, not all of these titles are journals per se but other kinds of serials, such as annual reports. So you'd need to be selective."

I quickly found the website for the *Journal of Public Affairs* and sent Stan the URL for its author submission guidelines.

"Thanks, Dave. Now, how about my other manuscript topic, transfer students?" Stan asked.

"Well, let's see," I said as I typed in *"transfer students"* into the library's list of journal titles. Nothing came up. I then did the same thing in the database where we found so much on service learning. However, all the results that came up were only annual report–type documents and not scholarly peer-reviewed journals.

"With this topic, we will need a different strategy. Since the term *transfer students* falls into the more discipline-specific area of education, let's use one of our education databases, ERIC."

As I quickly brought up ERIC, I mentioned, "ERIC has a thesaurus where we can find out if the term *transfer students* is actually a *subject heading*. Then we can go from there as we did in the previous database."

We both watched as ERIC came up, and then I clicked on the thesaurus tab and typed *"transfer students"* into its browse search engine. The first item on the top of a list of terms was *Transfer Students*, and I continued, "Ah, so it is a subject term in this database. Notice next to the two words is something called a *scope note*, which is the explicit definition for this heading. Therefore, for the ERIC database, *Transfer Students* means 'students transferring from one school or educational program to another.' Also, see that it continues with this note: 'If applicable, use the more specific term *College Transfer Students*.' My question to you is, does your article focus on college or other kinds of students?"

"No, it's only college students."

"Well, then you would not use the term *Transfer Students* but instead use *College Transfer Students*. I see that this term is listed next to the heading *Narrow Terms*. Since the term is blue-lined, by clicking on it, I get its own entry, including the following scope note: 'Students who have transferred or intend to transfer from one higher education institution or program to another to achieve more advanced or different educational goals.'"

"That's it. So what do we do now?" asked Stan.

I continued, "Well, let's copy the new term *College Transfer Students* and return to the search screen. I'll paste the new term into the first box and then change the drop-down menu to the right of the search box to read *DE Descriptors [exact]*. I could have used the broader search field called *SU Descriptors*, but since we know our subject heading exactly, we'll get better results and fewer false hits with the other one. Since you're interested in scholarly journals, I'll check the box next to the words *Peer Reviewed* and limit it to *Journal Articles* under *Publication Type*."

Again, Stan couldn't believe what he saw. "Wow, 125 articles, and they all look like they're from different journals. But how do I know which ones are for me?"

"Look here to the left of the entries. One of the limiting tabs says *Publications*. When I click on that, it ranks the top six journals out of these 125 articles, with the journal having the most articles at the top. I see that the first three journals have something to do with community colleges. I assume your research deals more with university student transfers, so you would likely be more interested in the fourth journal called, let's see, *Research in Higher Education*," I said as I clicked on that title.

Stan took up the conversation as the next screen came up. "Hmm, now we're talking about only five articles all from that same journal, *Research in Higher Education*, and pretty recent, between 2005 to 2009. Very nice."

"Yes," I said, "and you could go back and limit by the fifth journal title and so forth. You also get an idea of the kind of article related to your topic that successfully made it through the review process. In summary, the same process works for any topic by simply looking up a term in the thesaurus, searching by *SU Descriptor [exact]*, limiting by *Peer Reviewed* and *Journal Articles* and finally, after getting results, limit by publication title."

"Dave, you're magic. How can I pay you back?"

"Hah, nothing. Hmm, on second thought how about a nice e-mail to my associate dean?"

"You've got it." At that moment. his cell phone rang. He looked at the message and said, "Oh, I have to go; I'm needed back in my office. You've really been a lifesaver. Maybe you could come to our next faculty meeting and share this with the rest of our department?"

"Glad to do it. Just send me a time and place."

"Great. We'll be in touch."

And with that, Stan stood up and was soon hurrying out of the Gap passage. I just sat there, taking in the beauty of the place, the beauty of the moment. So this is how it feels to help another toward success: publish, not perish.

## REFLECTIONS

### Knowledge

* Go back through the reference interview and map out each search string, database, and limiting factors. Describe what you see as a pattern in the entire process.

- How long after Dr. Stanley Schoenleber told the librarian he needed to meet, did the librarian make an appointment? What does this say about providing reference service?
- What were the motivating factors that made Dr. Schoenleber meet with the librarian?

## Comprehension

- What was the main idea in this scenario? Hint: See the title.
- In the context of this reference question, explain what it means (or why it is important to know) that one journal title is held at more libraries than another journal title.
- Name two techniques that the librarian performed that could be defined as information literacy instruction. Remember: Information literacy is a set of abilities requiring individuals to recognize when information is needed and to have the ability to locate, evaluate, and effectively use the needed information. [2]

## Application

- Create a clear how-to-do outline using information from this reference transaction that can be published as a brief column in Brett College's next faculty newsletter with the heading "How to Find Your Next Journal to Publish In" (or something like that).
- Go to the blog for this book at http://referenceinterview.wordpress.com/, click the part for this chapter (Scenario 7—Helping Publish, Not Perish), and post your column idea for the next Brett College faculty newsletter (as composed for the previous bullet).
- What factors would you have changed in this scenario if such a faculty member approached you after a meeting for some journal ideas to publish in?

## Analysis

- Go to the ERIC database (http://eric.ed.gov/) and type *descriptor: "college transfer students"*—including quotations and the word *descriptor* followed by a colon (with no spaces), since we already know that this term is a descriptor (subject term). Also click the box next to *Peer reviewed only.* Compare the results you get with the results in this scenario's reference interview (the journals held at the most number of libraries) and make a brief comment.
- Make a flowchart to show the critical stages in this reference transaction.

- This transaction/interview had at least one tipping point (turning point) and maybe more. What was it, or what were they?

## Synthesis

- Create a library marketing campaign to reach out to faculty members at a university for increasing reference transactions and opportunities to share how faculty can implement information literacy with their students.
- Design a Web 2.0 site that faculty can use to find potential journals in which they could publish.
- Put new words to a known melody that illustrates this scenario. Tip: See http://www.youtube.com/watch?v=GNpNfhpqDk4.

## Evaluation

- Create a booklet about five rules that you see as important in this scenario. Convince others.
- Write an e-mail that will go to all the deans at a university describing the value of the campus librarians and their service in light of the benefits provided in this scenario.
- This reference transaction is not perfect. How would you have handled it differently?

## NOTES

Originally published in *Reference Librarian* in 2009: Dave Harmeyer, "Helping Publish Not Perish," *Reference Librarian* 50, no. 4 (2009): 413–18.

1. Ma Lei Hsieh, Susan McManimon, and Sharon Yang, "Faculty-Librarian Collaboration in Improving Information Literacy of Educational Opportunity Program Students," *Reference Services Review* 41, no. 2 (2013): 313–35.

2. Association of College and Research Libraries, "Information Literacy Competency Standards for Higher Education," January 18, 2000, http://www.ala.org/acrl/standards/informationliteracycompetency.

*Chapter Ten*

# Scenario 8

## *My So-Called Second Life*

Although it eventually lost popularity with educators when educational discounts were eliminated in fall 2010,[1] Second Life continues to be an engaging sandbox of seemingly endless three-dimensional fantasylands to explore and try out with a willing class of students. Selecting a generic avatar and name is just the start of a pastime that can end up costing real dollars if you want to, say, dress up your avatar, lease property, and build elaborate structures. The time when Second Life hosted X-rated sites, often near G-rated educational ones, is gone, which makes for a safer, saner experience for both newbie and veteran Second Life educators/librarians. Since late 2006 and early 2007, an amazing dedicated group of public and academic librarians created working libraries with free e-books, computer touch screens, and note cards that provided information about the learning space that your avatar was visiting. The libraries that have a presence in Second Life, some with information/reference desks, include Seanchai Library,[2] Rockcliffe University Library & Reference Center,[3] Community Virtual Library Reference,[4] and Stanford University Libraries.[5] The following scenario is an attempt at capturing some of this old wonder of doing a reference interview inside a three-dimensional digital experiment—something that may be re-created into the not-too-distant future.

## THE SCENARIO

I sit down at my private office desk and lift the lid off my favorite half gallon of mint chocolate chip ice cream. The carton had been sitting on my desk for

a quarter of an hour, and the inside edges of the cold stuff were just beginning to melt. I use a spoon to scrape the melted green and black-speckled
delight into my mouth.

I am celebrating. It is a late afternoon near the middle of August. The
K–12 students in the city would soon be back, finding their way to the
popular Richardson Public Library as one source for their class assignments.
Earlier that day during lunch at the Foothill City BBQ, the library's leadership team made some long-awaited decisions about reorganization. The temporary assignments given to me as interim director seven months ago had
been officially handed over to the new chairperson. Yes! I was now freer to
experiment with reference services in a new medium before mostly junior
and senior high school students started arriving at the reference desk. The
new, sometimes controversial, medium was the three-dimensional world of
Second Life.

The Richardson Unified School District took a student survey the previous spring. The results showed that 28.5 percent of the school students regularly found themselves in immersive, three-dimensional environments such
as World of Warcraft and Second Life. An additional 8.5 percent had registered avatars for such places.

However, Peter Wright, one of my Richardson Public Library colleagues
and our head of reference, was skeptical about these numbers. His words
kept rolling around in my head:

> Look, just because a group of students are spending some of their time in these
> places doesn't mean they'll use it for school work, let alone reference. I don't
> know, Dave. I think it's just a passing fad and not worth our time to invest
> with. I think efforts are better spent with other 2.0 tools like Facebook, Meebo,
> or our 24/7 reference service, maybe even Twitter. Besides, at the last National
> Library Association conference, there was quite a stir about Second Life, but
> few thought that it was really worth all the effort. Well, if you're really inter-
> ested, I suppose I'll support you dabbling in it. Do me a favor and keep me out
> of it, but do keep me informed.

So, I had my work cut out for me.

I scoop up another melting spoonful of ice cream while clicking on the
Second Life icon on my laptop's desktop. The screen turns black before a
small green revolving hand lets me know that the software is loading. My
recently upgraded laptop more than satisfied Second Life's computer requirements, which included installing a high-end graphics card. Having attended a couple of face-to-face and online Second Life seminars, I'd already
created an avatar. His name is Carpe Writer. From the seminars and dozens
of in-world visits, I'd come to know several library and educational applications created over the past couple of years. Thousands of hours had been
spent constructing virtual libraries, museums, and information resources in-

side the environment. However, today I am going in for another purpose: a reference interview.

The rotating green hand on top of the word *loading* morphs the black backdrop into a stunning coastal beach image showing off one of hundreds of otherworldly islands within the realistic, eye-popping Second Life graphics. [6] The words *Carpe* and *Writer*, presaved in log-in boxes, await my password that would unlock the magic. Just before my screen changes again, I glance up at the top right corner, taking notice of what greeted every Second Life resident as he or she entered: "Logged In Last 60 Days: 1,379,947" and "Online Now: 67,650."

My avatar's home spot is on Info Island near the Alliance Virtual Library. As my screen takes a few moments to construct the pixels of forms and objects near Carpe, I watch his bent-over Frankenstein-like figure come alive as if invigorated with electricity. Blurry images gradually come into crystal-clear focus, vivid and bright in the distance. Popping out of nothing, buildings, trees, fountains, and hills reveal stunning and rich images. Chirping birds are heard. As I move my keyboard's left-arrow key, my view turns 360 degrees, overlooking Carpe's head and revealing creative imagination that is both familiar and oddly unfamiliar at the same time. After all, it's only a bunch of zeros and ones on a server in California. Or is it?

I take another lick of ice cream to help ease my entry into the world of make-believe. Much less make-believe—but, for many residents, just as much a part of their real lives—is the in-world's economy, held together by a currency called Linden dollars, named in recognition of the original creators. By transferring U.S. or other currencies into and out of Linden dollars, residents can spend their bank accounts on imaginative accessories or outfits for special effects, such as wings accompanied by the sound of an occasional explosion, or on a new persona, such as a favorite cartoon character. I've taken the less creative and less expensive route for Carpe. His original newbie outfit is embellished with some free blue jeans, sandals, and a white western shirt with lace, and his face sports a chin puff, small mutton chops, and piercing blue eyes—my alter ego.

Avatar flying in Second Life is as simple as one click. Because flying is faster than walking or running, in moments Carpe is soaring in midair toward Alliance Virtual Library, one of dozens of library *sims* (or simulated objects) within Second Life. As Carpe approaches the library's reference desk, which is placed outside the building for added accessibility, I click on *stop flying*, and he gradually, clumsily, falls to virtual ground. I walk him behind the reference desk, poised and ready for virtual patrons and their questions. Covering the lower right part of my screen is a small rectangular map. If there were any avatar life forms within the range of a football field, they would be revealed as small green dots. The map displays five of these dots, most at a comfortable distance from Carpe. However, within seconds, one of the dots appears to be moving in his general direction. Orienting my view toward the northerly horizon, I can just make out a stick-looking figure at the end of the far-off plaza. Eventually, the outline of a darkly clad male avatar comes into view, growing larger and larger. He walks to within twenty feet of the desk and stops. As is true for all Second Life avatars, suspended above his head is a name, which reads *Manny Riel*. The environment allows for both texting and audio chatting, so I begin the conversation with Carpe in chat while I take another scoop of ice cream.

I type, "Hi, Manny. Welcome to Alliance Virtual Library. Do you have a reference question?"

The Manny avatar seems to be gaining its bearings as he adjusts a skewed stance and rotates toward my avatar's desk. He stops and becomes motionless for the second time. The dark figure then lifts up its arms zombie-like and begins a typing motion as if a keyboard were suspended in midair, the typical stance that avatars take when chatting in Second Life. The sound of typing is followed by a message in my chat window.

"Hi. Are you a reference librarian?"

I enthusiastically type Carpe's response, "Yes!"

"Then, yes, I do have a question of sorts," returns Manny.

While Manny is typing, I right-click my mouse on the avatar's image. A translucent circle with pie-shaped labeled sections appears near where I click. One choice on the ring is *profile*, which I click and in seconds read what day this avatar was created and which Second Life groups his owner had joined in-world, if any; it's a rather handy trick if you want to know a little about whom you are talking with. I was thinking, this avatar is relatively young, only a few months old, and had joined half a dozen in-world educational groups.

Manny's chat box continues, "I'm a professor at a community college and wanted to see for myself what applications there might be for teaching in Second Life."

Carpe responds, "Well, that's wonderful. I'm a librarian at a public library, but I can certainly show you some great examples. What field of study are you in?"

I wait as the Manny avatar raises his typing arms again, and the following text shows up in my box: "Physical sciences, physics, and I have some professor friends who teach history and literature."

"Great. Let me give you a brief rundown, and then let's teleport to one place. I could go audio, but I'll continue in chat so you can view the transcript later. Now, if you click on the *COMMUNICATE* tab in the lower left of your screen, you'll see our chat transcript, which you can copy and paste into another document."

"Sounds fine. Just let me know what I'm supposed to do. I'm no expert in this place," confesses Manny.

"Don't worry; we're all on our own learning curves."

Manny, a little relieved, says, "That's assuring."

In between digging out a few more spoonfuls of ice cream, I had Carpe quickly summarize what little I knew about education in Second Life, adding, "Librarians, educators, and many others have worked in Second Life for a number of years, creating hundreds of applications. There's a Second Life education wiki located at http://wiki.secondlife.com/wiki/Education. And I can't say enough good things about the Second Life educators' mailing list, called Second LifeED, which is linked from within the wiki site. Also, you'll find links to over 200 universities in-world and a couple of community colleges that have a Second Life presence."

Manny asks, "Sounds great. I've looked at the wiki but, really, what kinds of things do faculty do in Second Life?"

Carpe answers, "Well, just to name a few: office hours, classroom meetings for two, or large amphitheaters, which can hold sixty avatars at a time. Professors use in-world PowerPoint screens for lectures and supervise student art projects. Others have produced elaborate virtual archives, Star Trek–like holodecks, reconstructed lost historical sites, even whole civilizations. And some have made places where you can interact virtually with historically significant people. I could go on, but why don't I teleport us to one of these and let you see for yourself."

"Cool. You can do that?"

"Sure. Just right-click on my avatar and choose *add friend* on your radial menu. And I'll add you as my friend. This lets me teleport my avatar to a location and then request yours to follow. All you need to do is accept the teleport." I typed these details, thinking that he appeared to be pretty new and I wanted to make sure that he had as positive an experience as possible.

"I'm game," says Manny.

In a few moments we'd finished adding each other as friends. "We'll be going to a place that has to do with spaceflight. I'll teleport first and then ask you to join me. See you in a few seconds," I say, hoping everything would work out. In a few seconds, my avatar is whisked away to the new location, and soon I am requesting Manny to join me. I wait. A glowing light appears in front of my avatar and morphs into Manny. He has made it.

"Hey, Manny. You OK?" I query.

"Wow! That was interesting. So this is some kind of a space museum."

"Yep. It's not connected directly with NASA but has a lot of cool space-flight things. Get a note card by left-clicking on this icon." Note cards are ubiquitous in Second Life and are one way to explain the purpose of a location or object. In this case, we are at the International Spaceflight Museum. Specifically, we are two stories up on a large circular platform that the owners have labeled a rocket ring. Placed on the ringed platform are approximately fifty massive space rockets, most pointing skyward and all manufactured to scale. Each missile had its day in history years ago, but all are re-created here in all their original glory to be explored and gawked at in real time, something that's cost prohibitive in real life.

Manny seems excited as his owner types, "We have a space section in our general science course. Students could come here as a journaling experience."

I continue, "Maybe you're familiar with some of these rockets. Walk this way with me."

Manny answers, "Yikes, of course. This is *Saturn V* that took U.S. astronauts to the moon!"

And I join in, typing, "And here's the *Vostok 1*, the Russians' first man-in-space rocket."

Manny is about to make another observation, but there is a significant delay in his response. Something happened. He typed, "Hey, by the way, all of a sudden things got very dark for me. Did I do something wrong?"

At first, I could not figure out what Manny was chatting about, but then I remember, "Oh, not at all," I assure him. "You've timed out into your screen's midnight mode. Adjust back to midday. Here's what you do: in the upper left of your screen, click *World*, then click *Environment Setting* and then *Midday*."

The words "OK, that's much better" appear in my chat window—and then something unexpected, "I have something else I'd like you to know."

I wait, curious to what it is as the *tic, tic, tic* soon reveals the next message.

"You may have thought that I was a man. I'm not. I'm a woman."

I respond, "Oh, OK. No problem here."

The professor continues to chat through the Manny avatar, "When I first joined Second Life, my avatar was female. But I got so many passes that I got fed up and changed my looks to what you see now."

"Well, that's not surprising. I've heard Second Life described as a kind of a virtual Wild West. I guess some residents seem less inhibited when it comes to relationships, and others take advantage of that. This is probably something that needs to be kept in mind as your students come in-world for class."

Manny adds, "Anyway, let's continue. What else does this museum offer? My reference question is turning into quite an answer!"

High up on the rocket ring platform, the two avatars walk over to a small three-dimensional icon that looks like a planet with a rocket rotating around it. I explain that it's a teleport prompt for a rocket ride to outer space. In a few moments, our avatars are riding in a simulated rocket, complete with an elaborate control panel, engines blasting, and a window that looks out into dark space. As the ride completes, our avatars are placed on a wire mesh platform that appears as if it is suspended miles above in space, providing an astronaut's view of earth. Translucent signs direct us to look up at life-size models of the space shuttle *Endeavour*, the Hubble Telescope, and the International Space Station. I walk Carpe to the other side of the platform, where another sign, the size of a big-screen television, depicts the nine planets in our solar system (if you include Pluto), their moons, an asteroid belt, and a place to teleport your avatar to each planetary location as well as back on the ground. However, before I could explain this to Manny, who had clicked on her flying tab in an attempt to get a closer view of *Endeavour*, she is falling into the depths below.

She has just enough time to type, "Help!" Then the Manny avatar is gone from sight.

I'd fallen a few times myself from this platform, so I knew that after clicking *stop flying*, the fall would continue for a minute or so before reaching ground zero. No harm done to avatar or human, so I follow Manny to give her the instruction.

"Don't worry. Just click *stop flying*, and you'll be fine. Trust me."

In a few moments, we are back on *terra virtua* where Manny continues, "Wow! I thought I was a goner!"

I answer, "Yeah, I know, it's happened to me a couple of times. Something else, places like the Spaceflight Museum don't sustain themselves. It takes donations to keep it alive. There's a monthly fee that the owners pay for leasing the island, plus other costs. Think of what it would be like not to have such a place. If you know of any foundations or grant opportunities looking for innovative educational applications, this is the place."

We walk over to a space shuttle's robotic arm and play with its controls. We fly over a map of Cape Canaveral, complete with floating signs honoring the launching sites of well-known space flights. We finish by flying our avatars up and landing on a small platform suspended above the center of the rocket ring. Above this platform moves a solar system orrery. Here, we can take in the grandeur of the whole museum.

"Well, Carpe, this has been quite an answer to my original reference question. I suppose there are many more examples you could show me, but I have to go."

"No problem. If you're willing to give me your e-mail, I'll send you a couple of Second Life URLs, called *SLurls*, other places that you and your colleagues might find just as engaging as this place—for your students."

"Great. One more question. Where should I put my avatar?"

"Good question. It really doesn't matter since, when you log out, it disappears from others' views. Here is as good as any."

"OK, thanks. Look forward to getting those links. Bye!"

With that, Manny disappears from before my avatar. I then send Carpe back to Info Island and record one hour and five minutes of Second Life reference duty in my reference tally. My eyebrows rise in embarrassment when I notice that the half gallon of ice cream is now about half gone. I put the lid back on, walk out of my office into the staff lounge, and quickly slide my celebratory snack back into the freezer before calling it another day. So ends another experimental reference transaction in my so-called Second Life.

## REFLECTIONS

### Knowledge

- Why did the librarian enter Second Life? Why did the avatar Manny enter Second Life?
- How did the librarian find out that Manny had been in Second Life for only a few months?
- Why did the owner of Manny take on a male-looking avatar?

### Comprehension

- Define Second Life by what is explained in this scenario.
- What five or six things did the librarian give for Manny's question "What kinds of things do faculty do in Second Life?"
- Why do you think the librarian teleported the two of them to the International Spaceflight Museum?

### Application

- You must have known this was coming . . . register for a free Second Life account (http://secondlife.com/). There is an option for adding a credit card, which you do not need to do.

  - Before starting, check that your computer meets system requirements (http://secondlife.com/support/system-requirements/).
  - Download the latest version of the Second Life viewer (http://second-life.com/support/downloads/?lang=en-US).
  - Enter Second Life and, if this is your first time, you will be placed on Welcome Island, where tutorials teach you to move around.
  - When ready, go to one of the libraries mentioned in the scenario. Their SLurls (Second Life URLs) are in the scenario's endnotes. Copy and paste a SLurl into the Second Life viewer's address bar and go to that library.
  - Take a snapshot (click on the camera icon on the left or, in the top left corner, click *World*, then *Snapshot*). E-mail it to yourself or save it to your computer as proof of accomplishing this bullet.

- Go to the blog for this book at http://referenceinterview.wordpress.com/, click the part for this chapter (Scenario 8—My So-Called Second Life), and write a critique of this scenario. Extra credit: Find an information reference desk at one of the four libraries in Second Life, take a snapshot of it, then post it with a caption in this part of the blog.
- Give two reasons to do reference transactions in Second Life and two reasons not to.

## Analysis

- Identify one or more tipping points (turning points) that transacted in this reference interview.
- Make a flowchart to show the critical stages in this reference interview.
- In what two ways is this scenario similar to a face-to-face reference encounter? In what two ways is it unlike a face-to-face encounter?

## Synthesis

- Write about your feelings in relation to monitoring a reference service inside something like Second Life.
- Design a record, book, or magazine cover that illustrates one part of this reference interview.
- What kinds of problems does a reference service inside something like Second Life solve?

## Evaluation

- Design a three-question (or three-statement) questionnaire to be given to Second Life patrons to evaluate the librarian's reference interview effectiveness.
- Take one side of a debate on the viability of doing effective reference in environments like Second Life and create your talking points.
- Go back through the reference interview and judge the value of what the librarian did with Manny.

## NOTES

Originally published in *Reference Librarian* in 2010: Dave Harmeyer, "My So-Called Second Life," *Reference Librarian* 51, no. 1 (2010): 88–94.

1. However, these discounts were reinstated again on July 24, 2013; "Updated Pricing for Educational and Nonprofit Institutions," *Linden Lab*, July 24, 2013, http://community.secondlife.com/t5/Featured-News/Updated-Pricing-for-Educational-and-Nonprofit-Institutions/ba-p/2098039.

2. This library and the next three are located within Second Life. To visit requires a free Second Life account and the newest Second Life Viewer update; Seanchai Library (Second Life), http://maps.secondlife.com/secondlife/Imagination%20Island/78/191/26.

3. Rockcliffe University Library and Reference Center (Second Life), http://maps.secondlife.com/secondlife/Rockcliffe%20Library/48/215/23.

4. Community Virtual Library Reference (Second Life), http://maps.secondlife.com/secondlife/Imagination%20Island/172/210/28.

5. Stanford University Libraries (Second Life), http://maps.secondlife.com/secondlife/Stanford%20University%20Libraries/162/227/33.

6. Although still eye-popping, the descriptions of this Second Life experience were written in late 2009, so exact directions will not be the same in the current version of Second Life and its updated viewer.

## Chapter Eleven

# Scenario 9

*Reviving the Reference Interview: From Desk to Chat to Phone*

Perhaps one of the most dramatic shifts in the history of librarianship was the morphing of the reference desk into a kind of vague metaphor, like the water-pumping windmill, far less needed today but an iconic image of past success. It is a jarring realization that this foundation of the practice—always prominent and staffed with informed, friendly librarians—silently dissolved into a fraction of itself in just a few short years. Although a few of the largest academic libraries in the United States saw an increase in questions at the reference desk from 1995 to 2005, the majority witnessed a steep decline. [1]

One reaction to this disturbing reality has been to figure out why it happened. Although there may be other reasons, the main answer seems to be a shift in end user information-seeking behavior—library jargon for people preferring to find information on their own using the Internet and not librarians. I can just picture some reference librarians saying in their heads, "How dare people think they can get what they need on their own. Don't they know the Internet is littered with false information? We are the gatekeepers of accurate information!" Hmm, well, that may be true to some degree. The issue, if I may be so bold, is not misguided information users but librarians who are too prideful to admit that they are behind the times—who, like the proverbial frog in water being slowly brought to a boil, have lost connection with reality and are being cooked alive! Is it too late to do anything?

The following scenario illustrates another perspective—that the important thing is not necessarily that of preserving face-to-face interactions at a reference desk but rather embracing a renaissance, a reviving, if you will, of the reference interview. This new novel type of reference interview begins in one modality, face-to-face, but then transcends multiple forms, such as chat and phone, before there is a complete answer. This new process, by the way, is one that the Internet would be hard pressed to replicate.

## THE SCENARIO

When I arrived at Brett College, the Internet already had begun to take over. Nevertheless, convention dies hard in the library world, and several in-house initiatives occurred to save the reference desk. As the number of desk inquiries decreased, we looked for solutions to staff our outpost while the promises of online reference began to occupy more of our time. At first, we used well-trained and capable graduate student assistants, called *navigators*. They were to field questions and refer the tougher ones to the on-call librarian. The idea worked until we found out that even our most well trained were lured into the world of good intentions, failing to pass questions on to the professional. In addition, my on-call colleagues and I were far less available on call than what was practical. Our busy schedules added meetings that took us to places far from the reference desk and a reasonable response time.

The next attempt involved hiring, training, and supervising part-time employees as adjunct library faculty. These individuals often held master's or even doctoral degrees outside the field of librarianship. Adjuncts served on the desk during librarian meetings, late evenings, and weekends. Their added level of education brought to the desk a great sense of academic diversity. One scholar easily fielded requests for English literature criticisms of Beowulf, Shakespeare, Lord Byron, or Jane Austen, thanks to his background in comparative literature. Another, a Methodist pastor, became popular with our seminary students, as she skillfully used the theological collections as well as Greek and Hebrew syntax summaries and lexicons.

However, in less than a couple of years, our face-to-face reference statistics diminished substantially. This meant placing less focus on professional staffing at the physical desk and more on adapting toward newer technologies where, with some level of audacity, patrons were daring to take their questions away from library professionals yet expecting the same level of professional answers that had been delivered from the old reference desk.

So, today, it was late morning at my windowless office, and I was serving myself up a second cup of black coffee, anticipating that it would inspire me to finish up a few library personnel reports before lunch. Then my phone rang.

"Good morning. This is Dave speaking."

A nervous, rather loud female voice asked, "Where are you?"

The intensity of the caller's response threw me off a bit. Before I knew it, I barked back a knee-jerk "I beg your pardon?"

She continued in a more searching tone, "Ah, I mean, do you work at Brett College, or are you at some library call center? Are you a real librarian?"

A "real" librarian?! My mind began to shuffle through a number of thoughts: What has happened to our library benefactors, our strong patron base of support, that someone would greet me in such a way? Have things eroded that much? In library school, we studied how people's information-seeking behavior changed. As the Internet became ubiquitous and unlimited information was at everyone's fingertips, folks left the librarian out of the equation and sought information on their own, without a mediator or facilitator—thus, the term *disintermediation*.[2] My professors said nothing, however, about the loss of respect for librarians or the increase in rude patrons.

But wait a moment. What happened to the reference desk in the early part of the twenty-first century? Library science practitioners have sought out and located where the old familiar reference interview has moved to . . . it's called *online*. The physical desk is richly augmented with web-based technology tools, such as e-mail, chat, and online co-browsing. However, within these electronic global applications, people are no longer guaranteed to be served by librarians from their own library, and too often, the quality of those library experiences has disappointed, frustrated, or confused patrons. So just maybe they have a right to ask, "Who is answering my question? Are you a librarian, a student assistant, an adjunct nonlibrarian, or someone whom I will never personally know, at a call center in some faraway country?"

I tried to regain some composure as I answered, "Well, ah, yes. I'm a librarian. I have a terminal degree in librarianship, and I'm sitting in my office at Brett College. So, no, I'm not at some remote reference center, if that's what you mean." I still wasn't sure what this was about.

She lowered her voice to continue, "Oh, sorry, my name is Darleen, and you answered my question about the *Journal of Human Behavior and the Social Environment*."

I'd come to pride myself on being able not to go blank at the initial part of a reference interview. However, this time I did. My mind simply didn't process the journal title, because I was mildly disturbed that her name didn't register in my memory either. So I asked, "I did?"

Was I losing my mind? Darleen, Darleen . . . unique enough, but I couldn't recall her name.

She finally revealed an important detail, "Well, you e-mailed me yesterday. I have it on my screen. It was about the *Journal of Human Behavior and the Social Environment*."

Perhaps the coffee was starting to kick in. The journal title was now certainly familiar but not her name. Why? Then I connected the dots, "Oh yes, forgive me. You must have clicked on our Ask a Librarian Meebo on the library's website when we were not monitoring. And, yes, of course, I did answer you as I was getting ready to leave yesterday. How may I help you?" She continued to talk as I multitasked, clicking my laptop's cursor through a number of links on Brett College's 24/7 reference service archived transcripts. In a few moments, I had my previous response to her question on my screen. I now saw why her name never registered. She had left the name field blank.

She concluded, "So you are at Brett. I just need someone to help me find an article. I wasn't sure if I needed to come to campus to get it."

I could more clearly tell by comments in my e-mail response why she might have been confused. I continued to explain, "As you see in my original response, the journal you want is held at Brett in both paper and electronic. But it looks like the electronic full text is one year delayed. And you first had a chat conference with a librarian not at Brett. But it looks like that person gave you some relevant information. What exactly do you need?"

She answered, "Yes, you're right. I thought I was chatting with a librarian at my school, not someone in South Florida at a reference center or something."

I answered, "Well, a group of us at Brett do monitor the 24/7 chat during the daytime but not at a . . . let's see, it looks like you were chatting with a Frank around 12:40 in the morning."

"Yes, that's about right. My real question is . . . my professor said I needed to read one article from this journal. And I was on some webpage a few days ago and found a really good article on fathers and infants, but when I tried to get to the full text, it asked me to pay $35. I don't understand. I'm very frustrated. Do I need to come to campus to get it?"

I reassured her, "Well, it sounds like you tried to access the journal through the publisher's Internet site, and when you finally got a relevant article, a third-party vendor was happy to provide it to you at a cost. You do not need to do that as long as you're a student at Brett. We have it in full text without additional charges. Think of it as part of your tuition. You already paid for it."

"Wow! That's a relief. OK, so how do I get it?"

Over the next couple of minutes and a few more draughts of coffee, I walked her through how to get at the full text. "Darleen, what I'm going to do next is show you how to find the database that holds your article by using our web-based journal finder and then drilling down to the full text." In just a few moments, she was doing her own search on fathers and infants within the limits of the single journal title.

Our language soon turned to good-byes and thanks all around. The now pleasant-speaking student was grateful for the instruction and was even going to put in a good word for the library with her class.

"Thanks for your call, Darleen. Let me know if you need further assistance."

And with that, I hung up the phone. I got up from my desk and walked out of my office, through an outer area of other offices, and into the library proper. In a few moments, I was in view of the old wooden reference desk. It was during lunchtime, so it was unoccupied. Sentimentally, I moved behind it and sat in its double-armed swivel chair. It squeaked slightly as I scooted it under the desktop. I sat there pondering the previous conversation and wondered what future lie ahead for the old mainstay.

## REFLECTIONS

### Knowledge

- Was the patron Darleen justified in her tone of voice when calling the librarian? Explain.
- Make a chronological list of this reference transaction ending with the librarian's answer.
- How does the title of this scenario relate to the narrative?

### Comprehension

- What was the main idea in this scenario?
- Predict what Darleen might likely say to her class the next time she attends.
- Make a coloring book of the events as they unfolded in this scenario.

### Application

- List three professions where a customer would likely get an actual call center when trying to get service, as a way to see it from Darleen's perspective. Hint: Service contract for a refrigerator.
- Assemble a collection of photographs or images on one page and connect them by lines to demonstrate the different paths that this reference transaction took to completion.
- Go to an academic or public library's webpage that has a reference chat service (http://www.libsuccess.org/Libraries_Using_Specific_Types_of_Software_for_Embedded_Chat).[3] Click on the service to see if there is signage that tells the patrons that they may or may not get a librarian from that library. Describe your findings.

## Analysis

- Go to the blog for this book at http://referenceinterview.wordpress.com/, click the part for this chapter (Scenario 9—Reviving the Reference Interview: From Desk to Chat to Phone), and identify one or more tipping points (turning points) that occurred in this reference interview.
- If the first librarian that chatted with Darleen were able to provide her the answer, then this reference transaction would not have had so many twists and turns. What type of information would have benefited the chatting librarian to answer Darleen's question fully?
- At what point do you think the librarian demonstrated information literacy to Darleen? Recall: Information literacy is a set of abilities requiring individuals to recognize when information is needed and to have the ability to locate, evaluate, and effectively use the needed information.[4]

## Synthesis

- Imagine that you received a similar call from a patron. Write about your feelings.
- Can you think of other ways that the librarian could have dealt with Darleen's real question? Explain.
- If the reference desk is going away, what other new and unusual uses could you create for the desk that would remind patrons to ask librarians their research questions?

## Evaluation

- If Darleen were to evaluate her library service before calling the librarian, what do you think she would have said? What would she say after talking to the librarian?
- Devise three questions that Darleen could answer to determine if she is more information literate than before the reference interview.
- Go back through the reference interview and judge the value of what the librarian did with Darleen.

## NOTES

Originally published in *Reference Librarian* in 2010: Dave Harmeyer, "Reviving the Reference Interview: From Desk to Chat to Phone," *Reference Librarian* 51, no. 2 (2010): 163–66.

1. Brian Mathews, "While Reference Stats Decline, Oregon Surges +51%: A Glimpse at Some ARL Outliers," *Ubiquitous Librarian* (blog), http://theubiquitouslibrarian.typepad.com/the_ubiquitous_librarian/2008/12/while-reference-stats-decline-oregon-surges-51-a-glimpse-at-some-arl-outliers.html.

2. J. Stephen Downie, "Jumping Off the Disintermediation Bandwagon: Reharmonizing LIS Education for the Realities of the 21st Century," 2009, http://people.lis.illinois.edu/~jdownie/alise99/.

3. Meredith Farkas, "Libraries Using Specific Types of Software for Embedded Chat," *Library Success: A Best Practices Wiki,* February 18, 2011, http://www.libsuccess.org/Libraries_Using_Specific_Types_of_Software_for_Embedded_Chat.

4. Association of College and Research Libraries, "Information Literacy Competency Standards for Higher Education," January 18, 2000, http://www.ala.org/acrl/standards/informationliteracycompetency.

# Chapter Twelve

# Scenario 10

## A Reference Interview in 2025

I am pretty sure I'm within the mark when I say that if people did not have imagination, we would not have sustained heavier-than-air human flight, the electric light bulb, or the Internet. It's imagination that made Disney order the workers in Orlando, Florida, to build Cinderella's castle first, so that it became the point of focus as every other structure went up. Moreover, imagining the future has brought us such diverse science fiction genre from the minds of Jules Gabriel Verne to Clive Staples Lewis to Ray Douglas Bradbury. So why not take trends in librarianship and imagine the library only eleven years into the future. It's a way to give hope to the sustainability of the reference interview and the profession of library and information science. The scenario that follows attempts to be faithful to a couple of forward-thinking individuals with some effort toward imaging one idea of an academic library in the year 2025.

### THE SCENARIO

It was almost 11 pm, and Victoria, my twelve-year-old daughter, and I had just finished reading aloud "The Most Haunted House in England" from Dowswell and Allan's *True Ghost Stories* for her next seventh-grade book report.[1]

"Dad, that was so cool. Can we read another?" she asked between yawns.

"Well, sweetie, looks like we let the night get away from us. We'll continue after church tomorrow."

"Oh, alright," she said reluctantly.

"But first, let's answer one book report question: Who was the main character in this story?"

"That's easy," she piped up, "one of the ghosts, a French nun named Marie Lairre, who was strangled."

"OK, write that down and then off to bed."

As we readied for a restful night, I couldn't help but think what awaited me on Monday morning: my first meeting as chair of Brett College library's strategic planning committee. I had some ideas about improving our reference services in the next five years or so, but I was concerned that too many of my colleagues now believed that reference was a dying branch of librarianship.

"OK, brush your teeth, brush your hair, and be quiet so you don't wake up your sissy."

"Already done, Dad. And Diane's been sleeping for a while."

Whispering, I said, "Great. Sleep well and I'll see you in the morning."

I made my way down the dark hallway toward the master bedroom. As I got into my side of the bed, my wife's slightly turned head on her pillow confirmed that she was already slumbering . . . and in a very short moment, so was I.

Almost immediately, it seemed, I was awake again. Someone was vigorously nudging my arm.

"What's wrong?" I asked, thinking it was Victoria or Diane. However, it wasn't.

Oddly, the bedroom lights were on, and the person nudging my arm was very strange indeed. She appeared to be a woman in her late thirties, wearing a large black-rimmed Pilgrim-like hat, an oversized off-white collar, and a black cape adorned with large black buttons, reaching to the floor. My wife was nowhere to be seen.

"Thou art needed. Come with me, my good master" was all she said.

"Who are you, and what's going on?" I demanded.

"If thou canst play the game for a while and believeth, I am Marie Lairre on a mission, yes, with thou into the future, to meet the need of a reference patron."

"OK, this is way weird. Either I'm on some trippy dream—or maybe I'm dead," I protested.

"This reality is someone's destiny, my good fellow, and it is not yet known if thou wilt be found faithful."

"Ah, faithful? Faithful for what?"

"Thou wilt see."

My curiosity immensely piqued, I quickly dressed and hustled outside. My guide was already in the street, beckoning me to keep up with her. Odd how all the trees looked much larger than I remembered, and some of the houses were painted different colors. Am I really in a different time? It felt like midspring: puffy white clouds floated in blue sky, and the mountains to the north made up a mosaic of browns, greens, and purple cloud shadows.

We walked east, then north, via residential streets, eventually making our way to a crosstown thoroughfare. We boarded a bus, which looked more like a spacecraft than the public transportation I was used to seeing. Several people already were seated, reading newspapers or looking out windows. I remarked to my guide, "These folks are going to think that you're strange with what you're wearing."

"Only thou canst see me," she responded as she sat in a seat next to the aisle.

"Oh, that will come in handy," I muttered as I took my place next to a man reading a newspaper.

Now was my chance to see when this dream—or whatever—was taking place. The man was kind enough to let me look at some of his newspaper. The date read Wednesday, March 26, 2025. Yikes, if that's right, I'm eleven years into the future with a French time-traveling nun from the seventeenth century!

The bus arrived at my place of employment, Brett College; by this date, it would be something like a 126-year-old institution. We exited the fancy bus and walked onto campus. My guide was in front of me, showing me the way. We turned into the main part of what was referred to as the Old Campus (as the university grew, a second campus was developed to the northwest). We passed the School of Music and the School of Business buildings, and in front of us was the three-story Academic Center, home to undergraduate psychology and a welcome center. But I'd never seen so many people outside the building.

It was a massive beehive of activity, as people were going down covered escalators to a lower level of the building. The nun and I walked onto the moving stairs and were soon deposited onto a carpeted underground platform. To our right was an automatic sliding glass door that quickly opened to a shuttle train, the kind you might see whisking passengers among concourses in large airports.

The apparition spoke, "Godspeed, my master. I shalt see thee on the other side at the Athenaeum. But be observant." Then she walked onto an ascending escalator and soon shrank out of sight.

When the shuttle doors opened, I quickly walked inside the tube-looking vehicle, along with a group of students. I hung on to a strap hanging from the ceiling. The doors closed, and off we went. The "train" was called *The Red Trolley*, the same name as the old-fashioned gas-powered trolleys that once ferried students and faculty back and forth between campuses. But this vehicle seemed to be powered by electricity and traveled on cushioned rails. A trip that would have taken about ten minutes by the old trolley was finished in less than two. During these two quick moments, I retrieved a student newspaper from the floor. It confirmed the date, Wednesday, March 26, 2025. Inside, a notice described The J. L. Hedges Distinguished Lecture, "My Life in Digital Mediums: A Hopeful Journey." Another story reported that this spring semester marked the first time in the school's history that there were more online students (about 9,000) than on campus (8,000). And on the next page was an interesting article about a student who was attempting to "fast" from technology and get by with decades-old nonelectronic tools, such as a manual typewriter.

According to a digital readout scrolling just under the edge of the vehicle's ceiling, *The Red Trolley* had arrived at the Athenaeum, the midstop before its final destination at the Science Center. I got off the trolley and, after ascending an escalator, came upon a large plasma screen. It was a three-dimensional touch screen of the Athenaeum, a kind of library on steroids. After maneuvering with my finger a dozen or so parts of the structure, I soon learned that the state-of-the-art three-story building had opened only a few months before and replaced the three former campus libraries, which then were converted into campus offices and much-needed space for special collections. The underground area of the Athenaeum had a million-volume book capacity in compact shelving. Apparently, the book was still surviving in 2025. Ninety percent of the collection was closed to the public in something called *deep space*, but any item was retrievable within a fifteen-minute turnaround. Items also could be digitized within thirty minutes, made copyright compliant, and sent anywhere in the world. The rest of the books were current within five years and could be browsed by patrons.

The building was amazingly energy green, producing a significant positive carbon footprint. A combination of solar, wind, and even geothermal energy generators supplied all the energy needed for not only the facility but the rest of the university, with most of the energy coming from a geothermal well 450 feet below. But I had a job to do, so I made my way to the Athenaeum's place of reference, a large, round information/circulation/reference desk right in the middle of a noisy hubbub.

I was now on a spacious main floor and could see several other innovations. The facility was open 24/7 to meet the needs of every constituent. There was a child care area where children could be dropped off while moms and dads did research or attended classes. A food/coffee court took up about one quarter of the main floor, with the rest of this area broken into wide group work areas of multipurpose tables and chairs, all unified by a beautiful wood floor rather than wall-to-wall carpet (probably to ease the cleaning of spills). Scattered around second-floor balconies were treadmills and exercise bikes, some facing exterior windows; students here and there pedaled and trotted away. Everything necessary to complete a project was within an easy walk: graphic center, technology help desk, copier department, and the information/circulation/reference desk.

My guide had advised me to be observant, so I eavesdropped on a reference interview. Oddly, the event wasn't taking place at the big round desk but out near one of the group study areas. A woman I figured to be a librarian, standing next to an undergraduate, held what looked like a thin clipboard with a computer screen on it, something like an iPad. She was showing her clipboard screen to the student and explaining how to compose a search. I pretended to be waiting to ask her a question.

"I'll be with you in a few minutes." Then she continued, "And so your class project has multiple mediums to it. This means that you will use our search engine to find and create a mashup of text, speech, video, and still images, as well as the history of your interaction with other classmates and external experts. You will manage this within the constructivist portfolio for this class. Now, because some of your information will be tied to a couple of GPS devices, you'll need to build the architecture to capture that kind of data."[2]

I'm thinking to myself, so this is where reference is going? Multiple mediums and GPS!

She continued, "Since you don't have a brain tap, we'll just go with a voice-activated search. Let's begin with your first concept." And with a command-sounding voice, she spoke into her clipboard screen, "Maya's computer—search—compare models of strength-based student success."

Well, I thought to myself, I'm not going to have time to get a brain tap, whatever that is. How cool that you can now just talk into a computer and a search is activated.

The librarian continued, "And here are the results. They are ranked by an efficacy synthesis algorithm so that your outcomes are displayed in this table. It compares, let's see, 427 resources summarizing approaches, contracts along spectrums, and . . . look here, these five items have been automatically translated into English from Arabic, Chinese, and Spanish, including one audio file."

As I was taking it all in and wanting to ask a few follow-up questions, my nun guide reappeared and was walking toward me. "Thy destiny hath arrived," she announced as she pointed toward a college-age young man of Indian descent.

So, I took a deep breath, walked over to the man, and introduced myself, "Ah, excuse me, hi, my name is Dave. I'm one of the reference librarians. I understand you might need some help?" I said with a little trepidation.

"Well, I hope so," he said in perfect American English. "I'm a senior communication studies major, and I need some current and past Consumer Price Index housing information for my business class assignment."

"OK, that shouldn't be too difficult," I reassured him.

The student continued, "But you need to understand one thing. I know it might sound strange, but I'm on a technology *fast*. I suppose you could call it some kind of social experiment. I'm actually kind of excited about it. I got fed up with all the distractions in my life and wanted to have more intentional face-to-face time with friends and not be looking at a computer screen all day."

"Wow, that's admirable. Now that you mention it, there was an article in the student newspaper about you."

"Yeah, they took a picture of me using an old 1960s typewriter. I've also ditched my smartphone and computer and agreed to use a landline phone to keep in touch with family once a week. I even quit my IT student job."

"Well, let's see about your need. Of course, most Cataloging in Publication data are available online, but, you know what, I recall that there are some paper indexes that have the same information. Would it be OK if I find these titles using our online catalog?"

"Yes, that's fine. I just need the information in a book or newspaper form, not online."

Together, we went over to an open computer monitor to access the library's catalog search engine. Of course, there was no keyboard, and remembering what the other librarian just did, I spoke aloud in a commanding-type voice "consumer price index," and up came a number of sources sorted by date.

"This *CPI Detailed Report* won't do, because it's an online report," I said as I used my finger to scroll down the screen. "But I'm looking at this other one: *Handbook of U.S. Labor Statistics*; it's in an e-book format and in print. How far back do you need the data?"

"Well, I'm going back a couple of decades, so from, say, 2000 to today."

"Well, I think we can help you with that. The current reports would be down in open stacks, which I can show you in a moment. The older ones will be in our closed stacks called *deep space*. But we can get them in about fifteen minutes. Also, current Cataloging in Publication data are in the *Wall Street Journal* over by the newspaper racks, and last year's are also found in *Statistical Abstracts*, located behind the information/circulation/reference desk."

"That's great. I really didn't think it could be possible. I was thinking I'd have to stop the fast or take a lower grade. Thanks!"

"Sure," I said as I quickly found the call number for the volumes and placed an order for retrieval of the older ones from deep space. We then went down to the basement area and found the current volumes on the shelf. By the time we'd made it back to the main floor, the rest were at the main desk for him to check out.

As we said our good-byes, I noticed that the nun was hovering behind the student.

I moved over to her and whispered, "So, how'd I do?"

"Thou hast been found faithful and hast succeeded in the mission. Take hold of my garment and thy destiny shalt come to pass."

As I reached out to touch the nun's garment, everything around me turned into a blur and then darkness. The next thing I knew, someone was, again, vigorously nudging my arm. I woke up and found myself back in my bed, looking into the face of my daughter Victoria.

When she saw my eyes open, she quietly said, "Hi, Dad. You need to get up. It's morning!"

"What? Ah, well, yes, I suppose so. And guess what honey?"

"Yes, Dad?"

"You know that ghost story we read last night?"

"Sure do."

"Well, have I got a crazy dream to share with you!"

## REFLECTIONS

### Knowledge

- Why did the time-traveling nun ghost want the librarian to travel to the year 2025?
- How did the librarian first learn about the student who was fasting technology?
- Why did the clipboard-size computers not have keyboards?

### Comprehension

- What was the main idea in this scenario? Hint: Print.
- Explain three changes in the new Athenaeum that you would not have seen in the older academic library.
- Describe three innovations that were observed during the first reference interview.

### Application

- The student in the second reference interview could use print sources only. Name two that the librarian from the past knew about.
- The librarian from the past eavesdropped on a reference interview from the future. Examine the results and describe what was in the chart on the clipboard-size computer screen.
- Illustrate one other library innovation, reference or otherwise, that you predict will be available in 2025. Hint: Do a Google Scholar search.

## Analysis

- Go to the blog for this book at http://referenceinterview.wordpress.com/, click the part for this chapter (Scenario 10—A Reference Interview in 2025), and post one information literacy outcome that occurred in the first reference interview and one that occurred in the second. Reminder: Information literacy is a set of abilities requiring individuals to recognize when information is needed and to have the ability to locate, evaluate, and effectively use the needed information.[3]
- Name three problems that the librarian from the past had to overcome to successfully fulfill his mission: conducting a reference interview where the final resources were all in print formats.
- Compare and contrast the tipping points (turning points) in the first interview versus the second.

## Synthesis

- In this 2025 setting, the reference interviews were conducted mostly in the open space of the Athenaeum. Create and describe an alternative location where these interviews could have taken place that might have been more beneficial to learning. Hint: That is, improve on this model.
- Knowing what the reference interview might be like in the future (the first interview), which parts would you feel most uncomfortable with and why? Which parts would you feel most comfortable with and why?
- Defend or refute this statement: Best practices for conducting the reference interview rarely change; what changes are the tools and methods of delivery.

## Evaluation

- Make a statement about the librarian from the past that is true in light of the reference transaction and successful outcome.
- Devise two questions about conducting a successful reference interview in 2025 that you might want to ask the librarian of the future in this scenario.
- How might you improve the reference interview of the librarian from the past?

## NOTES

Originally published in *Reference Librarian* in 2010: Dave Harmeyer, "A Reference Interview in 2025," *Reference Librarian* 51, no. 3 (2010): 248–54.

   1. Paul Dowswell and Tony Allan, *True Ghost Stories* (Tulsa, OK: EDC, 2006).

   2. Peter Norvig, "Search in '2020 Visions,'" *Nature* 463 (2010): 26.

3. Association of College and Research Libraries, "Information Literacy Competency Standards for Higher Education," January 18, 2000, http://www.ala.org/acrl/standards/informationliteracycompetency.

*Chapter Thirteen*

# Scenario 11

*Hybrid Reference: Blending the Reference Interview and Information Literacy*

Why should information literacy be a part of the reference interview? Doesn't the librarian already have enough to do during the interview? I have a notion that with a little careful change in effort, information literacy can be covered during a reference transaction. According to the Association of College and Research Libraries, there are four parts to the "Information Literacy Competency Standards for Higher Education": recognize that information is needed, locate it, evaluate it, and use it effectively.[1] When student patrons initiate reference interviews (face-to-face, phone, e-mail, chat, etc.), there is an assumption that they are already fulfilling the first part, recognizing that information is needed, because professors have assigned papers that the students need to compose based on their topics. Locating relevant sources, the second part, is often a preliminary part of a reference interview, with the identification of the topic, the decisions about appropriate databases to search, the creation of one or more search strings, and the retrieval of the results.

The third piece of information literacy, evaluation, is covered as the record results are reviewed, sorted, and chosen by their citation and abstract information. If the results list calls for additional limitations (date range, scholarly/peer reviewed, full text, etc.), those are applied in succeeding search executions; but if a broader search is necessary, then Boolean OR or taking out part of the search string can fulfill this desire. Finally, the fourth component, effective use of the resource, includes giving attribution through class-required citation style—more broadly expressed as using information ethically. The following scenario presents an example of blending information literacy with the reference interview, including a simple four-quadrant rubric for framing the two as one.

## THE SCENARIO

It was the middle of spring finals week at Brett College, and, predictably, the reference desk was a time of feast or famine: I was either very busy or had little to record on my reference tally sheet. Looking outside the disciplined academic stronghold, I could see from my desk station the lofty foothills and canyons of the nearby mountains, beckoning me to daydream for one moment—ah, make that two.

I'd grown up near the college, and on such a day as today, after work my dad would take my younger brother, me, and a couple of the neighborhood kids on a short bike ride, training wheels and all, over to North Hills Park. After carefully locking our bikes to a dependable light pole, he'd lead the way to a well-kept forest trail that, in a half mile or so, took us to the treeless summit of the park's small wooded hills. We spent our hike telling one another tall tales about squirrels the size of bears or screaming at some poor stinkbug that'd made the unfortunate choice of traversing across our path. As our party emerged from the forest, *THE* event took placed. Somehow, my dad instinctively knew how to time the moment just right. The sun was just beginning to close in on the top-most ridge of the largest of the mountains some thirty miles northwest of us. We stopped and watched, catching our breath. To the southwest, at about the same distance, we could see a cluster of city skyscrapers, a grand icon of enormous human effort juxtaposed against the Creator's majesty of the setting sun. Pensively, we watched the ball of light reach the edge of jagged slopes, dissolve into a pinprick, and then leave us. In the dusk that followed, my dad led us down the slope, back to our bikes and civilization.

A pleasant-looking undergraduate female student, who smiled and looked at me expectantly, suddenly interrupted my reverie. My daydreaming evaporated as I quickly cleared my throat and asked, "Oh, hi. Can I help you with something?"

"Yes, please, I do hope so. My psychology professor has given us until the end of finals week to read two scholarly articles and summarize them. I haven't the foggiest idea how to get started."

"Well, let me see if I can help. If you don't mind, how about you come around to this side of the desk, and we'll look at the library's website together on my computer screen," I said as I slid out a nearby chair on wheels, pulled it next to me, and motioned for her to sit down. In the meantime, I was moving out of my e-mail screen and bringing up a browser whose home page was the site that I most often viewed: Brett College's library resources.

Even though psychology wasn't my liaison area, the question didn't seem to be too complicated. And let's face it, a librarian's ego is somewhat wounded if she or he doesn't at least try to answer the patron's question. Nevertheless, best practices tell us that if it's obvious that we will not fully address the question, then it should be referred to a discipline specialist. Referring, for me, however, is usually a tough call because it would likely delay the answer for the often impatient patron.

Another concept that's tempting to skip altogether during the reference interview is information literacy. If librarians don't regularly teach information literacy, then who will? Lately, I'd been more intentional with information literacy during reference desk times, and unless the patron seemed unusually rushed or the question clearly required a ready-reference answer, I'd settle in for a brief information literacy session, just as I proceeded to do with this interview.

I reached out and took one 3 × 5 card left behind from the library's bygone wooden card catalog days. Before turning it over, I noticed that it was a title card for a sixty-nine-page book on moths by Dorothy Childs Hogner, dated 1964. If nothing else, these information-finding tools from another era of librarianship come in handy as scrap paper! I began the session.

"Before we go to a database to find your articles, let me share what I'm about to do." I wrote out the word *keyword* on the top left of the card and *subject heading* on the upper right and explained, "I'd like to recommend that we start with one or more keywords on your topic, but we will eventually determine what the subject headings are for your terms. Using subject headings gets at better articles for your topic."

She commented, "OK, start with keywords and end up using subject headings." I continued, "Right. Also, when doing a search, two concepts are very important to remember; these are recall and relevancy." I wrote the term *recall* near the middle of the card and, under it, *relevancy*.

"You see, *recall* means the total number of items brought up when we do a search. And when you first start out using keywords, you usually get a large number of articles." With that, I put a line with an arrow going up (↑) to the right of the word *recall*.

"And *relevancy* means that, after a search, whatever comes up is viewed as useful for you; it's relevant to your topic. But usually when you first start out with a keyword, your results are not relevant, which I'd like to represent by an arrow going down." I then drew a down arrow (↓) to the right of the word *relevancy*.

"Don't get me wrong—I think Google and similar Internet tools are powerful free search engines, and I use them all the time. But often when you first start out using them with what essentially are keywords, you get lots of stuff (high recall) but often not very good stuff (low relevancy). However, the ideal for your particular search strategy would be results that are fewer in number (low recall) but very relevant (high relevancy)." I then drew a separate set of arrows to the right of the first set: an arrow going down ($\downarrow$) next to the first arrow and an arrow going up ($\uparrow$) next to the second. I then wrote *keyword* above the first vertical set of arrows and *subject heading* above the second vertical set of arrows and circled the second set.

"My goal is to get you toward the second set of arrows: you'll get fewer articles to look through but ones that are closer to your topic. Make sense?"

She answered, "Yeah, sure. I never really understood why I needed to spend so much time trying to find things using *subject headings*. I thought just typing in my topic would get pretty good results."

"Well, that's not always the case. Usually, keyword searches result in fewer hits that are useful. By the way, this technique of starting with key-words and working toward subject headings can be used for just about any topic in almost any database. So tell me, what is your topic?"

"Oh, well, that's just it, I don't have one. You see my professor left it kind of open-ended and said to just make sure we got two articles that were peer reviewed and to read the first eighteen pages of each."

"Well, at least it gives us something to go on. First, let's bring up a psychology database since this is the broader discipline for your assignment." I clicked on our A–Z list of databases, chose *psychology* under the pull-down subject category, and then clicked on PsycINFO. "PsycINFO is one of the more heavily used scholarly databases on psychology," I said as I clicked open to the database's search engine. "What's something you might be interested in?"

She thought for a moment and said, "Hmm, well, how about entertainment?"

"Great idea," I responded as I typed the word *entertainment* into the first search box. "What I'm doing is using your term first as a keyword. We also want all your articles to be peer reviewed, which can be easily done by checking the *peer-reviewed* box next to that selection. And I don't need to type the term *psychology*, because that's what this database is all about."

After clicking on *Search*, our results screen showed 1,454 items. "OK, now notice that on the left side of the screen, it says *Narrow results by*, with one of the categories labeled *Subject*. If we open up this section, it shows the top ten subject headings for all 1,454 of these articles. I see that the word *entertainment* is not listed here, so it's not a subject heading used within this database. But you see, so far we're still in the first set of arrows, high recall and low relevancy. We need to narrow the set of 1,454 articles. One way to do that is by changing the field indicator, which means changing the places that the search engine looks for your word. We'll change from *keyword* to, say, *title*. We could have used another field or even started over with another term as a keyword. But by looking for your term in the title, most, if not all, articles will have something to do with entertainment." With this, I changed the drop-down menu from *keyword* to *title* and clicked on *Search*.

"Notice that our results set is now significantly less at 182. It's getting better, lower recall and higher relevancy. More items on the screen are getting closer to what you want."

"Yes!" she said.

I continued, "Because we still have a relatively large number of items, I suggest that we limit by full text plus some other category. Let's see, oh yeah, look at this, you can limit by age." And with that, I clicked open a link that revealed six categories of ages. I continued, "How about articles that include studies on people in your own age group?"

"Sure. So, of these categories, that would be eighteen to twenty-nine years, right?"

"Ah, that's correct. And now let's see what we have," I said as I pressed the *Search* button one more time.

In a surprised tone, I said, "Well look at that, twenty-three articles. I think that's a manageable amount for this type of assignment, all scholarly full-text works that are about entertainment with eighteen- to twenty-nine-year-olds in mind. You can see here where the citation gives the page numbers. You can look at the ones eighteen pages and longer along with their abstract summaries. How's that?"

"Um, great, except, how do I get the full text?" she asked.

"Good question. Which article looks interesting?"

"Well, let's see, I like number 3."

"OK, the title is 'Explaining the Effects of Narrative in an Entertainment Television Program: Overcoming Resistance to Persuasion.'[2] Notice that this entry has a link to the full text right here," I shared as I clicked on the link and the full text of the article eventually filled the screen. "And whatever is on the screen, you can e-mail, print, or download it to a hard drive or thumb drive. Let's just send this to your e-mail." I proceeded to ask for her address as I brought up an e-mail screen with the article attached and then asked, "Did that answer your question completely?"

"Yes, it did," she said enthusiastically.

She found one other article that looked promising, and I e-mailed that one, too. As a way to wind down our session, I briefly summarized what we had done.

"Remember, this process can be used for just about any topic. Go into a database, first type in your term as a keyword and find out what subject headings might be used for your topic; if this does not work, try something else, like what we did, with the title example or come up with synonyms to your topic to use as keywords. Continue to narrow your search by peer review, age of subjects, date, full text, whatever, until you get a smaller set of results with high relevancy. Then start reading and choosing what you want.

If your results are too few, then add synonyms to your keyword search, expand on the date range, or even try another database. And please let me know if there is anything else I can help you with. Here's my business card."

As we said our good-byes and my time on the reference desk was finished, I noticed that it was just moments before the day's sunset. I got up from my comfortable padded chair and walked outside the library's cloistered walls into a gentle spring evening breeze. I looked up and watched the sun slowly descend on the same mountain summit that I had daydreamed about an hour ago. As the final moment came when that tiny yet still radiant spark of light slipped out of my sight, I felt a bit of an epiphany in the moment. As one day was ending to start yet another, I sensed that the classic form of referencing was easing toward a refreshing, newer blend of the librarian's interview with information literacy.

## REFLECTIONS

### Knowledge

- Why did the librarian focus on information literacy with this reference interview?
- Why did the librarian choose to answer this reference question even though psychology was not in his liaison area (area of expertise)?
- What was the behavior of the librarian when the student said she had no topic for her psychology paper?

### Comprehension

- Reproduce the arrow diagram and label it.
- Based on this reference transaction–information literacy attempt, use your own words to compose a definition of information literacy.
- What was the main idea in this scenario?

### Application

- Use the arrow diagram to demonstrate a reference interview result (step-by-step) with the topic of educational technology and the school library media center (K–12).
- Name two things that the librarian did that fulfilled one or more Reference and User Services Association's "Guidelines for Behavioral Performance of Reference and Information Service Providers."[3]
- Illustrate two factors that you would change in this reference interview.

# Analysis

- Go to the blog for this book at http://referenceinterview.wordpress.com/, click the part for this chapter (Scenario 11—Hybrid Reference: Blending the Reference Interview and Information Literacy), and post three information literacy outcomes that occurred in this scenario. Recall: Information literacy is a set of abilities requiring individuals to recognize when information is needed and to have the ability to locate, evaluate, and effectively use the needed information.[4]
- Write a brief biography of the student that was revealed during this scenario. Why is this useful?
- Describe one tipping point (turning point) in this reference interview.

# Synthesis

- Design a simple rubric that assesses the strengths and weaknesses of a librarian's ability to perform information literacy instruction during a reference interview. Hint: Use the "Information Literacy Competency Standards for Higher Education" as a guide.
- What would happen differently in this reference interview if the librarian had already met at least one other time with this student and went over the arrow diagram?
- Defend or refute this statement: Performing information literacy instruction during a reference interview is a best practice.

# Evaluation

- How would you have handled a student who just wanted you to give him or her two peer-reviewed articles and skip the information literacy instruction?
- Design a booklet about five rules that you see as being important from this reference interview–information literacy instruction.
- Choose one thing that you might suggest to improve the reference interview of this librarian.

## NOTES

Originally published in *Reference Librarian* in 2010: Dave Harmeyer, "Hybrid Reference: Blending the Reference Interview and Information Literacy," *Reference Librarian* 51, no. 4 (2010): 358–62.

1. Association of College and Research Libraries, "Information Literacy Competency Standards for Higher Education," 2000, http://www.ala.org/acrl/standards/informationliteracy-competency.

2. Emily Moyer-Gusé and Robin L. Nabi, "Explaining the Effects of Narrative in an Entertainment Television Program: Overcoming Resistance to Persuasion," *Human Communication Research* 36, no. 1 (2010): 26–52.

3. Reference and User Services Association, "Guidelines for Behavioral Performance of Reference and Information Services," May 28, 2013, http://www.ala.org/rusa/resources/guidelines/guidelinesbehavioral.

4. Association of College and Research Libraries, "Information Literacy Competency Standards for Higher Education," January 18, 2000, http://www.ala.org/acrl/standards/informationliteracycompetency.

# Chapter Fourteen

# Scenario 12

## *A Surprise at Rosey's Beauty Salon: Toward Ethos, Values, and Codes of Ethics*

There are rude and disrespectful reference staff out there. I suppose that's one reason why librarians have created clear, thoughtful guidelines, such as the "Code of Ethics of the American Library Association."[1] Although you may disagree, the code of ethics does give some form of a framework for conduct at point-of-service experiences, especially in the first code: "We provide the highest level of service to all library users . . . and courteous responses to all requests."[2] I find it egregious that a professional reference librarian would do any less. But they do.

The following scenario focuses partly on the fallout of a bad reference experience. It also illustrates another principle that slips under the radar of codes of ethics and expectations of library service conduct—that is, the attitude to be ready to exercise your reference calling, if you will, at a moment's notice, even in a beauty salon.

### THE SCENARIO

I was merely on my lunch break during my day-to-day library duties at Springdale Public Library, attempting to get a quick haircut before a couple of hours of reference commitment in the afternoon, when I had a rather unusual reference interview.

When I arrived at Rosey's Beauty Salon, down the street from the library in a refurbished small-town hardware store, my nose was immediately met with the fragrances of shampoos, hairspray, and mousse. On the back wall, a

wide-screen television was softly broadcasting the latest farewell season episode of the *Oprah Winfrey Show*. All three beauticians looked busy, hovering
over their customers, adorned in colorful capes protecting clothes and neck-
line from the thousands of hair shards falling harmlessly to the floor. Soon,
one of the hair stylists finished up and came over to the service counter. I was
inscribing my name on the clipboard when she asked a question.

"Are you ready?" she said between a few chews on a small piece of gum.

"Sure," I answered.

"Anyone you prefer?" I shook my head no.

"Okay, come with me."

Modestly dressed and in her midtwenties, she wore a pair of black jeans
and a matching black T-shirt with a set of delicate silver wings printed on its
back.

Chewing, she continued, "My name's Sandy. So, what can we do for you
today?"

I said, "Nice meeting you, Sandy, I'm Dave. I'd like 1 1/2 to 2 inches off
the back."

A little impatient, she responded, "So, what is it—1 1/2 or 2?"

"Oh, ah, 1 1/2," I corrected myself.

In a few moments, she draped me in my own multicolored cape and
started clipping off my requested 1 1/2 inches of hair. As she began to make
some customary small talk, she remembered noticing that I was wearing a
shirt embroidered with the public library's signature.

"So," she asked, "what do you do at the library?"

"Oh, ah, I'm, I'm a librarian," I said somewhat sheepishly.

"Really! I'm a student at Western Community, and our librarian was not
helpful at all. He was downright rude to me yesterday," she said in a con-
demning voice while waving a pair of scissors. Western Community was a
small rural community college about fifteen miles north.

I tried not to show my incredulous gasp and said, "That's awful. That's so
against our ethical codes of conduct. It's . . ." and I trailed off trying to think
of something to say that would turn the conversation around.

"Yeah, I'm doing this, you know, compare-and-contrast paper on J. P.
Morgan and Margaret Mitchell," she said in a matter-of-fact way. "This
librarian, he, he just kept looking at his computer and said, 'What do you
need?' And I said, 'Well, this is a library, isn't it? So I guess a book.' He
said, 'We probably don't have one on him, but here's two databases you can
try,' and I think he said, 'Gail and Eberhost' or something like that."

"Yes, I'm sort of familiar with those two. The first is Gale, and the second
is called EBSCOhost," I interrupted.

"Whatever," she said as she got out her electric clippers and began to trim
the back of my neck as I pointed my chin down.

She continued, "So, I'm kind of frustrated about librarians."

"I'm sorry you had such an experience. You know, it's just like, umm, how you treat your customers with respect. Most of the librarians I know work very hard at understanding what patrons want, giving them their full attention. It's what some might call our ethos or philosophy of empathy with patrons. There are even some written values, you know, codes of ethics that we're supposed to follow.[3] Anyway, if you don't mind me asking, when is your assignment due?"

"Well, let's see. My professor said we needed to e-mail it to her by this coming Sunday at noon."

"You know, I think I can help you," I said above the noise of the clippers, "if you need more information, that is." I was thinking to myself, could she take a break and maybe follow me over to the library?

"You mean right now?"

"Ah, no," I added. "Let's finish with the haircut first," and she continued to trim away.

I happened to notice something in the next stall over and asked, "Is that your laptop, and do you know if it's wireless here?"

"Sure, that's my computer and, yeah, our shop is wireless."

I was thinking, what have we come to? We're so wired it's even in our beauty salons.

"Great!" I continued, "Tell me again what your assignment is about."

She answered, "It's comparing and contrasting two historical figures from a list our professor gave out. I chose J. P. Morgan and the author of *Gone with the Wind*, Margaret Mitchell."

Soon, Sandy finished my haircut. As she swept up my 1 1/2 inches from the floor into a dustpan, I began to focus on her reference query. First, we worked a couple of minutes getting her laptop to come up, connecting to the wireless network, and authenticating her access to Western Community College's library database page. She clicked on the EBSCOhost link.

I said, "So, let's start by typing 'J. P. Morgan' into the first box. Now put quotation marks around him. Doing that will make this search look for his name as a phrase and help us find anything on him and not bring up false hits."

"That makes sense," she said.

"Hmm, no hits. Let's try this same thing in your library's online catalog. Click back a few pages and then on to the catalog." Again, she typed in his name as a phrase. What came up surprised both of us.

"Well, look at that," I said. "It's an e-book. You know, an electronic book. Your library must hold a subscription to one or more e-book vendors. Anyway, here, click on that link." Soon the entire book came up. It was about people and events in nineteenth-century American economy.

"Now, type his name in the search box for this book." What came up was a six-page chapter on the life of financier J. P. Morgan. Perfect! So, in some ways, I guess the librarian was correct. Her library did not hold a full book on Morgan, but it did have a chapter. And although I could be wrong, I doubt if Sandy could have discovered that by herself. She needed an information mediator, one who practiced the ethos, values, and codes of ethics of professional librarianship.

Going back to EBSCOhost with Margaret Mitchell as a subject heading, we found at least one brief article about her life. I think I impressed Sandy to no end. She couldn't believe her "luck" that one of her customers could so easily help her find the very sources that she needed to finish an assignment. Maybe librarians weren't that bad after all!

I paid Sandy for my haircut and added a tip as we said our good-byes. Exiting the door, I couldn't help think how a sense of commitment to a profession's ethos, values, and codes of ethics could serve one so well, even at Rosey's Beauty Salon.

## REFLECTIONS

### Knowledge

- What did the librarian at Western Community do that was unethical?
- What did the librarian from Springdale Public Library do first when he found out what the librarian at Western Community had done?
- How did the librarian from Springdale Public change the attitude of the beauty salon employee about librarians?

### Comprehension

- Compare the two librarians based on a code of ethics.[4] Hint: See note 4.
- Make a cartoon strip showing the sequence of events in this reference transaction.
- What was the main idea in this scenario?

### Application

- From the information given in this scenario, develop a set of ethical guidelines for reference librarians in your own words.
- Name two things that the librarian did that fulfilled one or more Reference and User Services Association's "Guidelines for Behavioral Performance of Reference and Information Service Providers."[5]
- If you were the supervisor of the reference librarian at Western Community College and you found out about his unethical behavior, how would you deal with it one-on-one? In a group meeting of library personnel?

## Analysis

- Go to the blog for this book at http://referenceinterview.wordpress.com/, click the part for this chapter (Scenario 12—A Surprise at Rosey's Beauty Salon: Toward Ethos, Values, and Codes of Ethics), and post a statement about the reference interview and code of ethics.
- Write a brief biography of the beauty salon employee/student that was revealed during this scenario. Why is this useful?
- Describe one tipping point (turning point) in this reference interview.

## Synthesis

- Design a simple rubric that assesses the strengths and weaknesses of a librarian's ability to perform an ethical reference interview. Hint: See endnotes.
- What would happen differently in this reference interview if the librarian at Western Community College had still been unethical but the student got the information she needed for her assignment?
- Defend or refute this statement: Reference librarians who do not comply with librarian codes of ethics should be fired.

## Evaluation

- Did the librarian getting a haircut perform any information literacy instruction in this reference interview? Explain.
- Write an appropriate e-mail to the supervisor of the librarian at Western Community College about what you learned from the beauty salon employee.
- Choose one thing that you might suggest to improve the reference interview of the librarian who received the haircut.

## NOTES

Originally published in *Reference Librarian* in 2011: Dave Harmeyer, "A Surprise at Rosey's Beauty Salon: Towards Ethos, Values, and Codes of Ethics," *Reference Librarian* 52, no. 3 (2011): 277–80.

    1. American Library Association, "Code of Ethics of the American Library Association," June 28, 1995, http://www.ala.org/advocacy/proethics/codeofethics/codeethics.

    2. American Library Association, "Code of Ethics," point I.

    3. Reference and User Services Association, "Guidelines for Behavioral Performance of Reference and Information Services," May 28, 2013, http://www.ala.org/rusa/resources/guidelines/guidelinesbehavioral.

    4. Reference and User Services Association, "Guidelines for Behavioral Performance"; American Library Association, "Code of Ethics."

5. Reference and User Services Association, "Guidelines for Behavioral Performance"; American Library Association, "Code of Ethics."

## Chapter Fifteen

# Scenario 13

## *The Reference Interview Thrives*

*Τ ὰ πάντα ῥ ε ῖ κα ὶ ο ὐ δ ὲ ν μένει* (tà pánta r̄eî kaì oúdèn ménei = everything flows, nothing remains still) comes from the Greek philosopher Heraclitus (circa 535–475 BC), but you probably know his saying best by the maxim *nothing is constant but change.* No one would argue that this is certainly the case in librarianship. Even before I finish typing this sentence, something else has likely changed in the profession! Do you remember National Union Catalogs? They are those rather large, mostly greenish 754 volumes (pre-1956) of pages containing mimeographed copies of hand-typed catalog cards produced since 1901 by the Library of Congress of its growing book collection, intended to help create local card catalogs around the United States and Canada. WorldCat and other bibliographic databases make National Union Catalogs less needed, even if there are concerns that there are titles not yet in WorldCat.[1] Anyway, this is a book about the reference interview. Question: Does it change?

Well, the mediums that the reference interview take place in have certainly been augmented—from face-to-face and phone to varieties of digital text-based formats and perhaps synchronous video or audio (and, for the adventurous, virtual environments such as Second Life). Nevertheless, have the principles of a successful interview changed? Based on the Reference and User Services Association's "Guidelines for Behavioral Performance of Reference and Information Service Providers," since the first guidelines were presented after 1992, changes have occurred.[2] One example is the 2004 addition of three categories, including the *Remote* heading providing advice for e-mail, chat, and phone domains, which lack the physical and verbal clues of face-to-face. But even for those changes, have the expectations in the interview actually changed? Perhaps this is something to take up in the blog (http://referenceinterview.wordpress.com/).

In the meantime, the following scenario illustrates change in the moving of a reference librarian from an urban/suburban academic library setting to a rural public one and examines differences, if any, in the reference interview.

## THE SCENARIO

I had never been east of the Colorado Rockies, so there was little in my past to go on for my first trip to the land of north-central Indiana. I had fallen for a pretty twentysomething named Hannah Miller, who worked twenty hours a week in the drama department at Brett College as choreographer, voice coach, and costume designer. Our paths crossed at the library reference desk when she came to get help on her master's thesis in special education, a program that she began virtually from her home state of Indiana. Brett's policy on faculty not dating students did not apply, so our mutual love deepened, and, on this maiden trip, I was to meet the parents and extended family.

Contrasting my first three decades of life in Southern California, I pretty much fell in love with the less hectic pace of life, authentic four seasons, and the ever-present Amish population of Indiana . . . the land of corn. Uncharacteristically, I got along well with my future mother-in-law, a woman of Swedish descent plus a sprinkle of American Indian. The rest of the clan seemed to tolerate my urban idiosyncrasies, such as my cloistering away to polish off a Grisham novel, my insistence on calling Highway 15 "the 15 freeway," or my radical loyalty to Dodger Blue when most garage interiors in the region were adorned with shrines to NASCAR's Dale Earnhardt.

The decision to move from SoCal to the Hoosier state was simple. We had been married all of four months when a call came in early April from the rural town of Springdale for an interview for the position of reference librarian at the area's only public library. On a whim, during the wedding preparations, I had turned in my résumé to this closest library to the Miller homestead, the Springdale Public Library. The distance was a mere six miles to what the locals called *The Pub.*

Having no mortgage and paying bills as they came due, we had no debt. So, despite an inevitably daunting transition from the West Coast to the Midwest, I accepted the job offer and we moved our life belongings during our so-called honeymoon summer. By the fourth of July, our temporary housing at the Millers' home—once the active hive of four daughters—took place in a younger sister's bedroom with a bathroom just across the hall.

One would think that the switch from an academic to a public library, unlike a move 2,000 miles across the country, would be a no-brainer. A library is a library, right? It soon became evident that this change was going to be more like a jarring paradigm shift than an easy segue into a new job—that is, except for one thing: the changeless, thriving reference interview.

For one thing, patrons were far more diverse than anything I'd imagine at Brett. Even though there was a well-kept, modern children's library downstairs in the original 1906 Carnegie library building, patrons at the main floor reference desk could be any age and certainly not all college students. The case in point was one of my first public library reference transactions. It all began when a soft voice with a noticeable lisp said, "Hi sir, my mommy told me to talk to you, sssssso it's OK."

I looked down from my barstool-high, somewhat intimidating desk (another change to accommodate to) and peered over my glasses at what looked like a girl of about four years in a yellow and white dress. Back at Brett College, I had become so comfortable with our normal-sized reference desk and the chairs on casters that our students used to slide around so that we could face the computer screen together.

She continued, "Do you have any *peepssss?*"

I looked around to see where her mother might be. No one nearby seemed to fit such a description. Of course, I had no idea what *peeps* were. My pride said, "Just Google *peeps* and see what comes up." But I remembered that a basic construct of this conversation was that of clarifying questions. If they worked on all other end users, why not this one?

I asked, "So, sweetheart, can you tell me a little more about, ah, peeps?"

A genuine smile revealed two missing teeth as she put her hands behind her back, began gently turning right and left, right and left, and in a lisp kind of voice shared, "He'sss round and yellow and hasss a red thing on his head. I learn all kindssss of sssssciencccccey stuff from him and hisss friendssss."

Now I was in familiar reference territory, with a clue of sorts.

More questions from the librarian. "Where do you see him, in a book or a video?"

"Video, silly."

And with that precocious confirmation, I was on the trail: a video with peep or peeps in it. I clicked on the library's online catalog, narrowed the search by video recording, and typed *peep**. Adding the asterisk allows the search results to include additional words with letters replacing the symbol, so *peeps* would be included. Up came thirteen results, and the first one was *Peep and the Big Wide World: Peep Figures It Out*. To the left of the title was a thumbnail image of the DVD's cover, sporting three animated characters, one in a round and yellow head/body and what looked like a red cockscomb on top. I turned the screen so that the little girl could see it.

She gave a little squeal, and began jumping up and down while repeating, "Yesss, yesss, yesss!"

Together we saw the next two records, *Peep Floats* and *Season Adventures*, to which my patron responded, "Oh, I've already sssseen the ssssecond one but not the otherssss."

After writing the names and call numbers on a slip of paper, I continued, "Great, I see that both videos are in the library. Just go downstairs over there, take this note to the lady at the desk, and she'll help you." By now, her mom had shown up and expressed her gratitude before the two headed for the stairs and, no doubt, hours of fun and learning.

A second area that surprised my assumptions about the similarities between academic and public library communities was the types of questions asked. Few patrons would require peer-reviewed resources, except for the occasional high school level of rigor. Another case in point . . .

It was a windy day, almost tornado-type weather, in late May. For a SoCal guy who could easily recall CNN's spectacular images of tornado devastation in the Midwest, I felt moderately safe with the knowledge that the old Carnegie library had survived this kind of weather for 107 years. In the late morning, a young man with the distinct Amish beard (clean-shaven upper and lower lip) and a wide-brim straw hat approached the reference desk. He spoke with some hesitation but with humility and respect.

"Good morning. I hope I'm not bothering you," he said.

I responded, "Oh, hi, no bother. How can I help you?"

Slowly, as if he had been practicing what he might say all morning, "I'm interested in any books you might have on raising geese."

During my less-than-a-year transplant from California to Indiana, I had been reading about the Amish's way of life. Their faith-based communities are a significant part of the Indiana rural makeup. As a rule, according to Miller and Aguilar (1984), "Amish ordinances (rules) . . . emphasize 'separation' from . . . 'government.' Inasmuch as public libraries are administered by non-Amish people and are tax supported government agencies, that might be sufficient cause to prohibit or discourage their use [by Amish]."[3] Nevertheless, some heads of households and unmarried sons and daughters of established Amish families do become public library cardholders and users.

Knowing that my patron would not have access to any technology that ran on electricity, I decided to go a classic route to teach information literacy. The library had a copy of the print version of the *Sears List of Subject Headings* in the reference section.[4]

As I was typing, I explained, "We have a book that you can use to find a book that we have on raising geese. Ah, here's the book's number: 025.49 SEA. The next time you visit the library, just go to this book to find any book on a topic, or come to the reference desk to get started."

As we walked over to the reference shelf, I described how the Dewey decimal system worked. I pulled *Sears List* off the shelf.

"OK, so let's look up *geese*." We turned to the term *geese*, which was followed by two numbers, 598.4 and 636.5. We walked over to where the first number would have been on the shelf, but no books were found. We then scanned the shelf for the second number and hit pay dirt. The young Amish man carefully pulled a book off the shelf, revealing its title: *Barnyard in Your Backyard: A Beginner's Guide to Raising Chickens, Ducks, Geese, Rabbits, Goats, Sheep, and Cattle.*[5] In that moment, we looked at each other, an Amish bonding with a non-Amish. Very cool.

Soon the young man with the straw hat was checking out a book that would meet his unique need, and another man returned to a reference desk, listening to the wind—a tornado-type wind—whistle around a 107-year-old library and thinking how, among such epic examples of change, the reference interview still thrived in the early part of the twenty-first century.

## REFLECTIONS

### Knowledge

- Make a simple list of three or four similarities and three or four differences between the first patron and the second.
- Although the scenario doesn't explicitly say so, why do you think the librarian expected there to be little difference between the academic library and the public library?
- Did the librarian conduct anything resembling information literacy during one or both scenarios? If so, please explain.

### Comprehension

- What is the main idea of this scenario?
- Go to the blog for this book at http://referenceinterview.wordpress.com/, click the part for this chapter (Scenario 13—The Reference Interview Thrives), and post a brief review of this scenario.
- Reread the reference interview with the second patron. Why did the librarian not show the patron how to find resources using a computer? What does this say about the reference interview just being a bunch of canned responses—that is, a series of premade responses for each part of a reference interview?

### Application

- Looking at both interviews from this scenario, what one or two things would you do differently as the reference librarian?

- Let's say that for the first interview, the librarian referred the girl to the children's reference desk downstairs on the basis of a policy for referring patrons to one reference desk or the other. Write a brief draft of that policy.
- With what you know about the reference interview in general, have the main ideas or principles for a successful one changed over the last twenty years or so? Please briefly explain with two or more examples.

## Analysis

- Make a bulleted list of three differences and three similarities between an academic library reference department and one at a public library.
- Identify the tipping point in each of these two scenarios. Remember: tipping point = that moment of the interaction where both librarian and patron know that what they are looking at is a promising answer to the question.
- From the information given about the two patrons in the scenario, construct a brief biography of each person. Why is this important when conducting a reference interview?

## Synthesis

- Design a record, book, or magazine cover illustrating each of these two reference interviews.
- Devise your own ways to deal with both reference transactions that are different from what the librarian did.
- Design a public library program, collection, or service that would increase collection usage and reference questions from a local Amish community.

## Evaluation

- If you took a job as a reference librarian in or near a population for which you were unfamiliar, such as an Amish community, what five steps would you take to prepare yourself for successfully interacting with this patron group?
- For any kind of patron (K–12 student, public library user, college student, adult learner), justify the kinds of preferred skills one would need to conduct a successful chat reference interview with a librarian.
- Judge and write about whether the librarian did an effective job of providing information literacy during the first and second reference interviews. What could he do, if anything, to improve information literacy in the future?

# NOTES

Originally published in *Reference Librarian*, in press: Dave Harmeyer, "The Reference Interview Thrives," *Reference Librarian* 54, no. 4 (2013).

1. John P. Abbott and Allan G. Scherlen, "National Union Catalog: Asset or Albatross?" *Proceedings of the Charleston Library Conference* (2013): 91, http://docs.lib.purdue.edu/charleston/2012/Collection/1/.

2. Reference and User Services Association, "Guidelines for Behavioral Performance of Reference and Information Services," May 28, 2013.

3. Jerome K. Miller and William Aguilar, "Public Library Use by Members of the Old Order Amish Faith," *Reference Quarterly* 23, no. 3 (1984): 322.

4. Minnie Earl Sears, *Sears List of Subject Headings*, ed. Joseph Miller (New York: Wilson, 2007).

5. Gail Damerow, ed. *Barnyard in Your Backyard: A Beginner's Guide to Raising Chickens, Ducks, Geese, Rabbits, Goats, Sheep, and Cattle* (North Adams, MA: Storey Books, 2002).

*Chapter Sixteen*

# A Conceptual Model for Online Chat Reference Answer Accuracy

The purpose of this study is to determine a research-based conceptual accuracy model of best practices for improving and appraising the service of library chat reference. The model draws on a statistical analysis of sixteen independent variables and their effect on one dependent variable: an accurate answer. Based on Pearson correlation and analysis of variance (ANOVA), the study analyzes two and a half years of archived data found within 333 randomly selected chat transcripts. The results provide a compelling model that, if applied, can improve the outcome of librarians who are working toward sustainable expertise in library chat reference and in the larger professional field of information and library science.

## LITERATURE REVIEW

A growing and popular technology in library service is virtual chat reference. Internet library patrons chat live with librarians, who then co-browse with the patrons toward web resources that provide answers to their questions. The extensive literature in professional writings on library reference, dating back to Samuel S. Green's 1876 article "The Desirableness of Establishing Personal Intercourse and Relations between Librarians and Readers," is unfortunately all too rich in anecdotal narratives, with little or no research to back up recommended practices.[1] In addition, the information and library profession lacks agreement in appraising the quality of the reference transaction, as Saxton and Richardson (2002) summarize: "After thirty years of research beginning with the two initial studies conducted separately by Charles A. Bunge and Herbert Goldhor in the late 1960s, the question of how to evaluate the quality of reference service remains unanswered. No widely accepted method for assessing reference service performance has been established."[2] The study in hand, however, addresses this void by suggesting a valid and original methodology designed to provide a theoretical conceptual model of best practices for the reference interview based on an empirical study of chat reference transactions.

There is an expectation by some library professionals that "transcript analysis could be used to enhance the effectiveness of reference librarians."[3] Nevertheless, because evaluation of chat reference is relatively new, most research for reference literature in general is still, as stated, more anecdotal than empirical. Wasik (2003) adds, "Until recently, very little attention has been devoted to the assessment of digital reference services, and much of the evaluation has been confined to digital reference tools and collections."[4]

However, attempts have been made to assess if reference chat transcripts of patron and librarian transactions follow known reference service models. Smyth (2003) used three library or research models for assessing reference and information services in a study of 143 chat transcripts at the University of New Brunswick.[5] Specifically, transcripts were studied to see if the following three models were present: Katz's question types as modified by Sears (called Sears's classification of reference question types), the Association of College and Research Libraries' literacy competency standards, and the Eisenberg-Berkowitz information problem-solving model (also known as Big6). Smyth found that none of the models completely explained what took place within the chat transaction. Interestingly, it was discovered that important components of each model fell outside the actual reference chat interview. For example, based on the Association of College and Research Libraries' five literacy competency standards, the transcripts appeared to include the following three standards: standard 1 (determine the nature and extent of information needed), standard 2 (access needed information effectively and efficiently), and, occasionally, standard 5 (understand the economic, legal, and social issues surrounding the use of information and access the use of information ethically and legally).[6] However, the functions of standard 3 (evaluate information and sources critically and incorporate into knowledge base and value system) and standard 4 (use information effectively to accomplish a specific purpose) were assumed to take place outside explicit interaction with the virtual librarian.

Driver (2003), although not investigating chat reference as such, performed a quantitative and qualitative analysis of forty-three MBA chat room participants, looking at the development of three behaviors: shared meaning, skillful discussions, and the creation of individual as well as collective mental models about group interaction.[7] Even though the study was exploratory and not generalizable to a target population, it provided a starting point for studying the chat environment as a place for skillful discussions and as a place to apply mental models.

Radford (2003), in a Virtual Reference Desk Conference presentation, summarized the analysis of forty-four chat transcripts submitted to Library Systems and Services' Samuel Swett Green Award for Best Virtual Reference Transcript contest, using criteria developed for evaluating contest submissions as well as the theoretical framework of Watzlawick and colleagues (1967).[8] Two of the criteria questions included "Are open-ended questions used at the outset of the initial interview to clarify the information needed?" and "Is the question answered correctly?" The Watzlawick framework provided a guide to distinguish between content and relational aspects of the transactions. Highlights of Radford's detailed visual analysis of all forty-four potentially award-winning transcripts yielded the following noteworthy data from the librarian's side of the chats:

- 86 percent ($n = 38$) exhibited "rapport building" and 73 percent ($n = 32$) offered reassurance.
- 77 percent ($n = 34$) provided closing rituals and 57 percent ($n = 25$) provided greeting rituals.
- 23 percent ($n = 10$) evoked "compensation for lack of nonverbal cues" in the form of emoticons (11 percent, $n = 5$), repeated punctuation such as *!!!* (7 percent, $n = 3$), and ALL CAPS (5 percent, $n = 2$).
- 5 percent ($n = 2$) used abbreviations (e.g., *LOL*).[9]

Hirko (2004) produced an online manual of checklists designed to evaluate virtual chat reference transcripts.[10] Although the results of the project were described in anecdotal language with no statistical analysis, one of the checklists helped validate the instrument used in the present study. A two-page Virtual Reference Transaction Checklist operationalized twenty constructs grouped into five headings, including the following three: Setting the Tone, Getting the Question Straight, and Keeping Me Informed.

Sloan (2002), in a Virtual Reference Desk Conference presentation, discussed using word frequency analysis software to evaluate reference chat transcripts.[11] Sloan used Bell's free frequency index software tool on Georgetown University's website.[12] When text is placed in its processor box, the web-based tool creates a list of the top twenty most frequently occurring words/symbols. Sloan found the following top ten words (singular or plural) from 877 chat transcripts: article ($n = 146$), book ($n = 111$), journal/magazine ($n = 109$), library ($n = 95$), paper ($n = 70$), APA/MLA/bib/cite ($n = 68$), online ($n = 46$), research ($n = 38$), source ($n = 36$), and student ($n = 30$).

Kwon (2004)—in a Virtual Reference Desk conference presentation, later published as an article in *Reference and User Services Quarterly* with Gregory (2007)—found ten measurable Reference and User Services Association behaviors for the online chat environment, of which six were statistically significant for user satisfaction when present versus when they were absent.[13] With a subsample of 422 transactions out of 1,387, Kwon coded reference success by averaging the scores of four user satisfaction questions on a survey taken by patrons after the transaction. The six behaviors with statistically significant differences based on $t$ test—that is, the six that received higher user satisfaction when present than when absent—were as follows: patron's name used ($p < .05$); listening ($p < .01$), as scored by the presence of receptive communication; searching for or with patron ($p < .001$), as scored by the presence of the librarian showing this behavior; pointers ($p < .001$), as scored by the presence of the librarian providing information sources; "Answered?" ($p < .001$), as scored by the presence of the librarian asking if the question was answered and if the patron needed more information; and "come back" ($p < .05$), as scored when the librarian stated, "If you need further assistance, please contact us again."[14] Kwon also conducted a multivariable regression analysis and found the following five behaviors as significant predictors of users' satisfaction (listed from strongest to weakest): asking whether their question was answered completely (regression coefficient $\beta = .181, p < .000$); providing pointers, such as search strings and useful URLs (regression coefficient $\beta = .124, p = .014$); asking patrons to come back when they need further assistance (regression coefficient $\beta = .112, p = .019$); searching with or for patrons (regression coefficient $\beta = .112, p = .023$); and listening (regression coefficient $\beta = .097, p = .044$).[15]

In addition to the Smyth study (2003), a number of studies apply or look at different modeling theories in relationship to the reference transaction. Richardson (1999) used a systems analysis approach for explaining the reference transaction process, identifying fifteen functional requirements necessary for successful question negotiation, and created diagrams and flowcharts to illustrate the fifteen findings.[16] Cottrell and Eisenberg (2001) applied the aforementioned Big6 model to categorize reference transactions, providing trends data.[17] Although looking at asynchronous digital reference (e-mail), Pomerantz, Nicholson, Belanger, and Lankes (2004) took a survey-based approach to evaluate the paths that digital reference services take and so validated the general process model of this kind of reference.[18]

Finally, Saxton and Richardson (2002) provided one of the most comprehensive studies of the face-to-face reference transaction by building four types of models from an analysis of sixteen independent variables' effect on four dependent variables, based on multiple regression and hierarchical linear modeling.[19] The four concluding models were as follows: the complete model (the Reference and User Services Association behavioral guidelines are a good reference practice and provide high-quality service for librarians who follow it), the useful model (patrons find useful information when helped by librarians who follow the Reference and User Services Association guidelines and when the patrons' education level is high), the satisfy model (patrons are most satisfied when helped by librarians who follow the Reference and User Services Association guidelines and have high professional behavior), and the accurate model (answers are most accurate for queries of low difficulty).[20]

## METHOD

The current study unobtrusively analyzed 333 randomly selected academic reference chat transcripts from 2,500 archived records that transpired at one university's chat service over a two-and-a-half year period from March 13, 2003, through August 31, 2005. The study looked at sixteen independent variables (see table 16.1) and their effect on the single dependent variable of an accurate reference answer. It measured only the outcomes of answer accuracy and did not analyze the variables' effect on other reference outcomes, such as utility (the usefulness of an answer) or user satisfaction.

An analysis of the 333 chat transcripts gave evidence that 120 virtual reference librarians at 43 U.S. institutions of higher education conducted reference interviews with over 320 remote patrons, with each user accessing the service through the library website of one Southern California undergraduate and master's-granting university. The total enrollment at this university in September 2004 was 19,804 (full-time equivalent, $n = 16,603$). In the 2003–2004 academic year, its library holdings included 755,671 volumes and 5,153 journal title subscriptions.

Data collected from the content analysis of the 333 transcripts were evaluated by Pearson correlation (for those independent variables with numbers) and ANOVA for all variables, using the statistics software package SPSS. In addition, for independent variables that were numbers, quartile frequencies were determined to run with ANOVA, a methodology used in behavioral and educational research.[21]

The seventeen variables used in the study (except number of URLs, type of question, and answer accuracy) were initially derived from the Reference and User Services Association's guidelines and then operationalized from a literature review described in the fourth chapter of my 2007 dissertation.[22] The dependent variable, accuracy of an answer, was adapted from Richardson and Reye's (1995) eight-point accuracy scale.[23] Since their scale was interpreted implicitly as interval data, the current study also applies this scale as interval, so the range of responses chosen by the analysts is recognized as continuous and the distance points on the scale are approximately equal. Each score for accuracy of answer is defined in table 16.2 (8 = high accuracy, 1 = low accuracy), with the terms in the far-right column signifying the service quality as labeled by Richardson and Reyes.[24]

**Table 16.1.  Study Variables**

| No. | Description | Title | Measure |
|-----|-------------|-------|---------|
| | Independent variables | | |
| 1 | Librarian's initial contact time | Hold time | Seconds |
| 2 | Total time of transaction | Service time | Seconds |
| 3 | Longest time gap by librarian | Time gap | Seconds |
| 4 | URLs browsed with the patron | Co-browsed | Count |
| 5 | Keystrokes by librarian | Key librarian | Count |
| 6 | Keystrokes by patron | Key patron | Count |
| 7 | Keystrokes by both | Key both | Count |
| 8 | Question's difficulty | Difficulty | Seven-point scale |
| 9 | Librarian response "Are you there?" | "Are you there?" | Present/absent/NA |
| 10 | Librarian's friendliness | Friendliness | Present/absent/NA |
| 11 | Lack of jargon | Jargon | Present/absent/NA |
| 12 | Use of open-ended questions | Open-ended | Present/absent/NA |
| 13 | Use of closed and/or clarifying questions | Closed | Present/absent/NA |
| 14 | Objectivity | Objectivity | Present/absent/NA |
| 15 | "Question answered completely?" | Completely? | Present/absent/NA |
| 16 | Type of question | Type | Six categories |
| | Dependent variable | | |
| 17 | Accuracy of answer | Accuracy | Eight-point scale |

Note: NA = not applicable.

## Sampling Procedure

In an effort to generalize findings to the target population and not include chat sessions tested by librarians or incomplete transcripts due to training, the sampling was taken from the most current records available (August 31, 2005) and extended before the target university's first year's use of the service, determined to be sometime in January 2002. Therefore, the transcripts used for the study were conducted from March 13, 2003, through August 31, 2005, and numbered approximately 2,500.

The sample size needed to represent a population of 2,500 is 333, with an error rate of 5 percent and a degree of confidence of 95 percent.[25] During pilot samplings, it was found that up to 55 percent of the transcripts included nonrespondents (incomplete transcripts) or minors (i.e., those likely under the age of eighteen). Assuming a 55 percent worst-case scenario, 740 tran-

**Table 16.2.   Answer Accuracy**

| Score | Analysts' Qualitative Judgments | Service Quality |
|-------|--------------------------------|-----------------|
| 8 | Librarian referred patron to a single source with an accurate answer. | Excellent |
| 7 | Librarian referred patron to more than one source, one with an accurate answer. | Very Good |
| 6 | Librarian referred patron to a single source does not lead directly to an accurate answer but served as preliminary source. | Good |
| 5 | Librarian referred patron to more than one source, none leads directly to an accurate answer but one which served as a preliminary source. | Satisfactory |
| 4 | No direct accurate answer given, referred to another person or institution. | Fair/poor |
| 3 | No accurate answer, referral given (e.g., "I don't know"). | Failure |
| 2 | Librarian referred patron to a single source which did not answer the question. | Unsatisfactory |
| 1 | Librarian referred patron to more than one source, none answered the question. | Most unsatisfactory |

Adapted from Richardson and Reye's (1995, 240) eight-point scale.

scripts were therefore randomly selected out of 2,500 to achieve the necessary 333 (i.e., 45 percent of 740). Randomization was accomplished by accessing the website random.org and generating 740 random numbers between 1 and 2,500, displayed in nine columns. For the sake of confidentiality and Institutional Review Board policy for exempt status, all personal information (names, phone numbers, e-mail addresses) for both patron and librarian was deidentified before coding.

## Coding Procedures

Two levels of coders were used for the project. The first level included four university student assistants who coded the seven quantitative variables for each of the 333 transcripts. Coding was simplified by a student-designed macro program for Excel that used time stamps in the transcripts to determine hold times, service times, the longest time in seconds between librarian posts, as well as the number of keystrokes (including spaces) by librarian, patron, and both for each transcript. URLs were counted by hand.

The second level of coders (called analysts) included three academic reference librarians with similar reference experience (myself and two librarians at two other academic institutions) who coded the nine qualitative independent variables and the dependent variable for each of the 333 transcripts. Analysts coded accuracy of answers along an eight-point scale (table 16.2); question difficulty along a seven-point scale; type of question by six categories (research question, library technology, ready reference, request for material, other, bibliographic verification); and seven additional librarian behaviors as present, absent, or not applicable. Behavior coded as not applicable met two criteria: first, it was not found in the reference transaction; second, and more important, it was judged inappropriate for that transaction. This is different from simply absent, which connotes missing behavior appropriate for a reference transaction. Analysts were paired into three teams (AB, BC, AC) for interrater reliability. Each analyst was then assigned 222 transcripts to code from the randomly selected 333 according to the following scheme: AB coded transcripts 1–222; BC coded transcripts 112–333; and AC coded transcripts 1–111 and 223–333.

For both a pilot run of nine transcripts and the first twenty to thirty coded transcripts, I talked through discrepancies among analysts until reaching agreements on interpreting coding for each variable. Interrater reliability was determined by Pearson correlation among three pairs of analysts on the question's difficulty—namely, because this variable contained the largest number of rater discrepancies as well as point differences in mean scores and standard deviations out of the total seventeen variables. The top three discrepancies were as follows: question difficulty ($n = 186$ discrepancies, 56 percent, $M = 0.82$, $SD = .916$), answer accuracy ($n = 75$, 22.6 percent, $M = 0.38$, $SD = .794$), and open-ended question ($n = 67$, 20.2 percent; nominal data—thus, no point differences in means and standard deviations). Because all three pairs of analysts had Pearson correlations above .60 for the question difficulty variable, rater reliability was determined to be strongly related: raters 1 and 3 were most similar ($r = .831$), followed by raters 2 and 3 ($r = .784$) and raters 1 and 2 ($r = .662$).

## FINDINGS

With the purpose of establishing a conceptual model of online chat reference accuracy, the study found thirty incidences of significance among nine of the original sixteen independent variables and chat reference answer accuracy. Seven variables did not exhibit a significant effect: hold time (the time the patron waits for the librarian to begin a chat), the librarian's response to the patron's "Are you there?" statements, the number of URLs co-browsed, the librarian's sense of friendliness, the librarian's lack of jargon, the librarian's objectivity, and the type of question asked. The nine variables that did exhibit a significant effect on answer accuracy are discussed under four categories: *librarian interest* (i.e., librarian demonstrates interest in patron's question)—

for longest sustained time gaps by librarians and service time; *question nego-tiation*—librarian's use of open-ended questions, librarian's use of closed and/or clarifying questions, and whether the librarian asked if the question was answered completely; *keystrokes*—by librarian, by patron, as well as by both; and *question difficulty*. Two transcripts were removed from the study because one was a duplicate and one contained a conversation with a minor.

## Librarian Interest

The first of two behaviors under *librarian interest* deals with the longest sustained time gap by the librarian during a reference transaction. The mean value of librarian chat gaps was 3.8 minutes ($SD$ = 4.0 minutes, $n$ = 331, minimum = 0 minutes, maximum = 55.6 minutes, next maximum = 19.5 minutes, skewness = 7.33). The data for this variable are highly skewed due to at least one outlier (55.6 minutes) with most time gaps clustered around the mean. Upon closer observation, the extreme outlier was due to the librarian waiting a long time before adding at least one more chat posting after the patron had disconnected. The data point was retained because it appears that this behavior (librarian continuing the chat for an amount of time, sometimes quite long, after the patron has finished) occurs in a number of transcripts (the next five outliers generated gap variables of 10.5, 18.2, 16.5, 16.3, and 14.4 minutes). In addition, in the chat environment, librarians often continue the chat as they gather additional information beyond the concluding response of the patron, knowing that the finished transcript will be sent to the patron's e-mail (if given) and that it often contributes greatly to the quality of their final answer. For this study, such behavior is considered a part of the sustained time gap variable as well as the reference transaction as a whole.

Pearson correlation was conducted between the total number of longest sustained time gaps by librarian and answer accuracy scores ($r$ = −.113, $r^2$ = .012, $p$ = .04), demonstrating a significant correlation between librarian time gaps and an accurate answer. A shorter time gap is related to a higher accuracy score. However, only 1 percent of the variance in answer accuracy is accounted for by the longest time gaps; thus, there is a weak relationship.

ANOVA with time gap found a statistically significant $F$ ratio ($F$ = 3.51, $p$ = .016). An ANOVA-based Tukey honestly significant difference (HSD) post hoc test was run with time gap variable quartiles. It found that for the .05 level, chat reference transactions with librarian gaps in the first quartile of 1.85 minutes or less produced a significantly higher accuracy mean than chats with librarian gaps in the second quartile of 1.87 to 2.83 minutes (accuracy mean difference = .691, $p$ = .022) as well as in the fourth quartile of 4.47 minutes or more (accuracy mean difference = .648, $p$ = .038). There was no significant difference found with the third quartile ($p$ = .394).

The second variable under *librarian interest* is service time, the total time of each chat transaction. For service time, the mean value was 16.0 minutes ($SD$ = 11.73 minutes, $n$ = 331, minimum = 1.9 minutes, maximum = 91.5 minutes, skewness = 2.261). Pearson correlation was run between the total service times of all transcripts and answer accuracy scores ($r$ = −.143, $r^2$ = .02, $p$ = .009). This demonstrates a significant correlation between service time and an accurate answer. A shorter service time is related to a higher accuracy score. However, only 2 percent of the variance in answer accuracy is accounted for by service time; thus, there is a weak relationship.

ANOVA with the service time variable found a statistically significant $F$ ratio ($F$ = 4.97, $p$ = .002). An ANOVA-based Tukey HSD post hoc test was run with service time variable quartiles. It found that for the .05 level, chat reference with service time transactions in the first quartile of 8.3 minutes or less (half the average service time of 16 minutes) produced a significantly higher accuracy mean than service times in second, third, and fourth quartiles between 8.32 and 13.08 minutes (accuracy mean difference = .807, $p$ = .005), 13.1 and 20.75 minutes (accuracy mean difference = .735, $p$ = .012), and 20.77 minutes and greater (accuracy mean difference = .704, $p$ = .019).

## Question Negotiation

The first of three behaviors under *question negotiation* is open-ended question, where the librarian asks an open-ended type question to "encourage the patron to expand on the request or present additional information."[26] The three analysts disagreed on this category 20.1 percent (67 transactions, $n$ = 333) of the time when coding transactions, so these data points were counted as ambiguous. The remaining data show librarians using open-ended questions 33.6 percent of the time ($n$ = 112). In addition, in almost half the cases (45.3 percent), either the librarian did not use an open-ended question ($n$ = 75, 22.5 percent) or the analysts determined that the patron's question did not require one for an answer ($n$ = 76, 22.8 percent).

ANOVA with the open-ended question variable found a statistically significant $F$ ratio ($F$ = 3.881, $p$ = .009). An ANOVA-based Tukey HSD post hoc test was run with the open-ended question variable data. It found that for the .05 level, those transactions determined by analysts to be not applicable for librarians to ask open-ended questions (and the librarian did not ask an open-ended question) produced a significantly higher accuracy mean than those transactions where librarians did ask open-ended questions (accuracy mean difference = .727, $p$ = .009). When this ANOVA analysis was run again filtering out the sixty-seven ambiguous categories, significance improved from .009 to .006 with the same accuracy mean difference of .727. These data show that when the patron's question is not applicable for an open-ended question (and one is not asked), the librarian is likely to give a significantly more accurate answer than that for the transaction where the librarian does ask open-ended questions. Open-ended questions should not be asked unless the patron's question calls for it.

The second of three librarian behaviors under *question negotiation* is closed-ended and/or clarifying question used "to refine the search query."[27] The three analysts disagreed on the closed-ended question category only 13.2 percent of the time, so those cases were coded as ambiguous. The percentage of transactions where librarians used closed-ended questions was 55 percent. In about one-third of the cases (31.2 percent), either the librarian did not use a closed-ended question ($n = 48$, 14.4 percent), or the analysts determined that to do so was not applicable ($n = 56$, 16.8 percent). When ambiguous cases were removed from the analysis (a total of forty-four transactions where analysts disagreed), ANOVA with the closed-ended question variable did find a statistically significant $F$ ratio ($F = 3.003$, $p = .051$, but $p = .048$ for the ANOVA post hoc test). When ambiguous cases were filtered out, an ANOVA-based Tukey HSD post hoc test showed that for the .05 level, when the patron's question was not applicable for a closed-ended question response (and a closed-ended question was not asked), the librarian was likely to give a significantly more accurate answer than that from the librarian who does not ask closed-ended questions and should have (accuracy mean difference = .740, $p = .048$). This means that the librarian will more likely give an accurate answer by not asking the closed-ended question unless the patron's question explicitly calls for it.

The third and final behavior under *question negotiation* is the so-called follow-up question, where the librarian "asks the patron if his/her questions have been completely answered."[28] Analysts disagreed on coding for this variable only 16.8 percent of the time (56 cases). The follow-up question was asked in 37.5 percent of the cases. Almost half (45 percent) did not contain the question (not present, 12.6 percent), or analysts determined that to do so would have been unnecessary (not applicable, 32.4 percent).

ANOVA with the follow-up variable found a statistically significant $F$ ratio ($F = 10.631$, $p = .000$). An ANOVA-based Tukey HSD post hoc test was run with follow-up data (minus the fifty-six ambiguous records). It showed that for the .05 level, chat reference transactions with the follow-up question got a higher accuracy mean than did those transactions where analysts judged that the follow-up behavior was unnecessary (not applicable) and the librarian did not ask it (accuracy mean = 1.109, $p = .000$). This means that librarians get higher accuracy by always asking the follow-up question even if to do so seems unnecessary or awkward.

## Keystrokes

Pearson correlation was run for all three keystroke variables (librarian, patron, and both) and answer accuracy scores: librarian ($r = -.126$, $r^2 = .02$, $p = .022$), patron ($r = -.146$, $r^2 = .02$, $p = .008$), and both ($r = -.146$, $r^2 = .02$, $p = .008$). This demonstrates a significant correlation between keystrokes and an accurate answer. For all three, fewer keystrokes are related to a higher accuracy score. However, only 2 percent of the variance in answer accuracy is accounted for by *each* of the three keystroke variables (or 6 percent for all three); thus, there is a weak relationship.

ANOVAs for the three keystroke variables found a statistically significant *F* ratio for all three (for librarian keystrokes, $F = 2.814$, $p = .039$; for patron keystrokes, $F = 2.917$, $p = .034$; for both, $F = 2.970$, $p = .032$). Quartile frequencies and an ANOVA-based Tukey HSD post hoc test found, at the .05 level, statistical significance between the number of keystrokes and answer accuracy mean scores for all three keystroke variables (librarian, patron, both). The industry standard for measuring e-mail keystrokes is as follows: one line of text = seventy-four monospace characters (i.e., using a font like courier, which maintains the same space length for each typed character).[29] Using this standard of seventy-four characters per line of text, librarians who keystroked 6.5 lines of text or less are more likely to answer questions accurately than those who keystroked 15 lines of text or more (accuracy mean difference = .647, $p = .041$). Interestingly, the librarians, on average, typed twice as many keystrokes as did patrons: librarian mean = 12 lines of text, or 886 keystrokes ($SD = 605$); patron mean = 6 lines of text, or 433 keystrokes ($SD = 367$).

## Question Difficulty

The last category of independent variables having a statistically significant effect on answer accuracy in 333 chat reference transcripts was *question difficulty*. This construct was coded along a seven-point scale ($1$ = low difficulty, $7$ = high difficulty). Descriptive statistics show that 166 (50.2 percent) of the patron questions were judged as being low difficulty (coded as 1.0–2.0), with the majority of the questions (82.8 percent) falling below medium difficulty (4.0) and only a small amount (6.6 percent) being judged as high difficulty (5.0–8.0).

Pearson correlation was conducted between the total number of question difficulty scores and their answer accuracy scores ($r = -.403$, $r^2 = .162$, $p = .000$), demonstrating a significant correlation between question difficulty and an accurate answer. Lower question difficulty is related to higher accuracy score. The analysts' coding also exhibited 16 percent variance in answer accuracy accounted for by question difficulty; thus, there is a strong relationship.

ANOVA with the question difficulty variable found a statistically significant $F$ ratio ($F = 7.286$, $p = .000$). Not surprising, an ANOVA-based Tukey HSD post hoc test, at the .05 level, found the easy question categories to result in statistically higher accuracy means than those of the more difficult questions (for difficulty levels 1 and 4, accuracy mean difference = 1.712, $p$ = 001; for difficulty levels 1 and 5, accuracy mean difference = 2.325, $p$ = .009). Interestingly, the range of low answer accuracy means occurs at relatively low levels of question difficulty (2.0 and 2.5) when compared to very easy questions (1.0 and 1.5). This means that very easy questions are more likely to result in higher answer accuracy, but accuracy begins to suffer even for moderately difficult questions and not just for the medium to high difficulty questions.

## DISCUSSION AND CONCLUSION

Out of sixteen independent variables, this study found the following nine exhibiting a significant effect on chat reference answer accuracy, based on Pearson correlation and ANOVA: longest sustained time gaps by librarians, service time, librarian's use of open-ended questions, librarian's use of closed and/or clarifying questions, librarian asking if the question was answered completely, number of keystrokes by librarian, number of keystrokes by patron, number of keystrokes by both librarian and patron, and question difficulty. The culmination of these results builds toward a new conceptual model of online chat reference with the focus on answer accuracy, along the following eight-point rubric: keep short gaps between chat responses, maintain a short total transaction time, type less not more, expect to type twice as much as patrons, ask closed-ended questions when appropriate, closed or clarifying questions are preferred, ask the follow-up question, and know that moderately easy questions can decrease accuracy.

The first of eight points in the model is to maintain shorter time gaps between sending responses to patrons. According to the study, shorter gaps increase answer accuracy. This principle also reinforces the Reference and User Services Association's behavioral guideline of librarian interest, particularly section 2.3.2, keeping the librarian's time away from the patron short and maintaining word contact to reinforce interest.[30] Although the extreme outliers for the gap variable may have skewed quartile results for this study, it is useful to remember to keep gaps to no less than one and a half minutes because anything around two minutes or higher is likely to decrease answer accuracy.

The second part of the model requires maintaining a shorter total transaction time with the patron, which increases answer accuracy. This reminds me of a mathematician and librarian from India, Ranganathan, and his fourth law of library science, "save the time of the reader."[31] This precept of the model also affirms two additional Reference and User Services Association guidelines: 1.3.2, "responds in a timely fashion to remote queries," and 2.3.1, "acknowledges user questions in a timely manner."[32]

Under the topic of a shorter time sequence is an interesting phenomenon that occurs at a particular point along a time continuum in the reference transaction. It seems to echo the economics law of the point of diminishing returns. Once this point is reached, the librarian is less likely to get an accurate answer and is wasting the time of the patron. The sensible librarian who does not find the answer within a reasonable time refers the patron to another person, institution, or service that may lead more effectively to an accurate answer. Findings from the study suggest that chat librarians need to keep transactions to within eight minutes. Transactions beyond eight minutes decrease accuracy, which seems to occur quickly just after the eight-minute threshold. Therefore, the average time of 16 minutes per transaction found in the study is too long for gaining accurate answers.

The third research-based practice for the model regards keeping keystrokes to a minimum. The behavior of keeping things brief is a trend found in the study. Virtual reference software vendors may find it profitable to test if this principle works by adapting the librarian's interface to record in real time not only the number of keystrokes but also time during the transaction. If one uses the standard of seventy-four monospace characters per line of e-mail text, then the study suggests that virtual librarians need to keep keystrokes per total transaction to within six to fifteen lines of text. Anything over fifteen or so will decrease accuracy. Any text, by the way, copied and pasted into the transaction would not count as keystrokes, nor would script messages.

The fourth component in the model's rubrics informs the librarian that he or she should expect to type twice as many keystrokes as the patron. This surprise finding in the study revealed that for every keystroke typed by the patron, the librarian returned twice as many. This kind of online dance appeared even across each quartile segment between librarian and patron.

The fifth idea of the model cautions the librarian from beginning the question negotiation segment of the reference interview with an open-ended question. Unless the nature of the question explicitly calls for one, an open-ended question unnecessarily decreases answer accuracy. Answer accuracy in the virtual environment is improved if there is patience in waiting for a time when such a question is more appropriate.

The sixth piece recommended in the model is the practice of asking closed or clarifying questions but only when appropriate. If the librarian asks a closed-ended question when the interview does not call for it, answer accuracy decreases.

As a seventh principle in the model, freely ask the follow-up question, "Does this completely answer your question?" Librarians will get higher accuracy by asking it.

The eighth and last design of the conceptual model is to know that even moderately difficult questions decrease answer accuracy. Although very easy questions are more likely to generate accurate answers, findings show that questions right above the least difficult begin to quickly decrease answer accuracy. Perhaps this awareness will avert the presumption that only difficult questions decrease answer accuracy.

The primary purpose of this study—to offer a research-based conceptual model of best practices for improving and assessing virtual chat reference service—has been achieved. It is hoped that many who practice chat reference as a part of their responsibilities will apply the findings of this study and thrive. In so doing, each can continue to contribute to the sustainability of the field of library and information science and compassionate, dedicated service to the patron/end user.

*Author note: The author deeply appreciates the many editorial and content recommendations from his three dissertation committee members, Margaret J. Weber (chair), Farzin Madjidi, and John V. Richardson, Jr., throughout the process of creating this one of two Findings chapters for his dissertation* Online Virtual Chat Library Reference Service: A Quantitative and Qualitative Analysis, *2007, Pepperdine University.*

## NOTES

1. Samuel Swett Green, "The Desirableness of Establishing Personal Intercourse and Relations between Librarians and Readers," *American Library Journal* 1, no. 1 (1876): 74–81; John V. Richardson, "The Current State of Research on Reference Transactions," *Advances in Librarianship* 26 (2002): 175–230.

2. Matthew L. Saxton and John V. Richardson, *Understanding Reference Transactions: Transforming an Art into a Science* (San Diego, CA: Academic Press, 2002), 3.

3. Corey M. Johnson, "Online Chat Reference: Survey Results from Affiliates of Two Universities," *Reference and User Services Quarterly* 43, no. 3 (2004): 238.

4. Joann M. Wasik, "Digital Reference Evaluation," para. 2, June 30, 2003, http://www.vrd.org/AskA/digref_assess.shtml.

5. Joanne Smyth, "Virtual Reference Transcript Analysis: A Few Models," *Searcher* 11, no. 3 (2003): 26.

6. Association of College and Research Libraries, "Information Literacy Competency Standards for Higher Education," 2000, http://www.ala.org/acrl/standards/informationliteracy-competency.

7. Michaela Driver, "Improving Group Learning through Electronically Facilitated Skillful Discussions," *Learning Organization* 10, no. 5 (2003): 383.

8. Marie Radford, "In Synch? Evaluating Chat Reference Transcripts," paper presented at the Fifth Annual Digital Reference Conference, San Antonio, TX, November 17–18, 2003,

http://www.vrd2003.org/proceedings/presentation.cfm?PID=231; Paul Watzlawick, Janet Beavin Bavelas, Don D. Jackson, and Bill O'Hanlon, *Pragmatics of Human Communication: A Study of Interactional Patterns, Pathologies, and Paradoxes* (New York: Norton, 1967).

9. Radford, "In Synch?"

10. Buff Hirko, "VET: The Virtual Evaluation Toolkit," 2004, http://vrstrain.spl.org/textdocs/VETmanual.pdf.

11. B. Sloan, "Asking Questions in the Digital Library: Can Users Define a VR Service?" paper presented at the Fifth Annual Digital Reference Conference, Chicago, 2002, http://www.vrd.org/conferences/vrd2002/ proceedings/sloan.shtml.

12. Cathy Ball, "Web Frequency Index," 1996, http://www.lextutor.ca/freq/eng/.

13. Nahyun Kwon, "Assessing Virtual Reference Success Using 2004 RUSA Behavioral Guidelines," paper presented at the Sixth Annual Virtual Reference Desk Conference, Cincinnati, OH, 2004, http://www.vrd2004.org/proceedings/; Nahyun Kwon and Vicki L. Gregory, "The Effects of Librarians' Behavioral Performance on User Satisfaction in Chat Reference Services," *Reference and User Services Quarterly* 47, no. 2 (2007): 137–48.

14. Kwon, "Assessing Virtual Reference," slide 18 (PowerPoint); Kwon and Gregory, "The Effects of Librarians' Behavioral Performance," 144, 145, table 1.

15. Kwon, "Assessing Virtual Reference," slide 20 (PowerPoint); Kwon and Gregory, "The Effects of Librarians' Behavioral Performance," 145.

16. John V. Richardson, "Understanding the Reference Transaction: A Systems Analysis Perspective," *College and Research Libraries* 60, no. 3 (1999): 211–22.

17. Janet R. Cottrell and Michael B. Eisenberg, "Applying an Information Problem-Solving Model to Academic Reference Work: Findings and Implications," *College and Research Libraries* 62, no. 4 (2001): 334–47.

18. Jeffrey Pomerantz, Scott Nicholson, Yvonne Belanger, and R. David Lankes, "The Current State of Digital Reference: Validation of a General Digital Reference Model through a Survey of Digital Reference Services," *Information Processing and Management* 40, no. 2 (2004): 347.

19. Matthew Saxton and John V. Richardson, *Understanding Reference Transactions: Transforming an Art into a Science* (San Diego, CA: Academic Press, 2002).

20. Saxton and Richardson, *Understanding Reference Transactions.*

21. Elise A. Fillpot, "A Study of Selected Variables Associated with Freshman Attrition at the University of Iowa [PhD diss., University of Iowa, 2004]," *Dissertation Abstracts International* 65:4486; Kenneth Harold Smith, "The Effectiveness of Computer-Assisted Instruction on the Development of Rhythm Reading Skills among Middle School Instrumental Students [PhD diss., University of Illinois at Urbana-Champaign, 2002]," *Dissertation Abstracts International* 63:3891.

22. Dave Harmeyer, "Online Virtual Chat Library Reference Service: A Quantitative and Qualitative Analysis [PhD diss., Pepperdine University, 2007]," *Dissertation Abstracts International* 68/10.

23. John V. Richardson and Rex B. Reyes, "Government Information Expert Systems: A Quantitative Evaluation," *College and Research Libraries* 56, no. 3 (1995): 240.

24. Richardson and Reyes, "Government Information Expert Systems," 240.

25. Jack E. Edwards, Marie D. Thomas, Paul Rosenfeld, and Stephanie Booth-Kewley, *How to Conduct Organizational Surveys: A Step-by-Step Guide* (Thousand Oaks, CA: Sage, 1997), 63; Robert V. Krejcie and Daryle W. Morgan, "Determining Sample Size for Research Activities," *Educational and Psychological Measurements* 30 (1970): 608, 609.

26. Reference and User Services Association, "Guidelines for Behavioral Performance of Reference and Information Services," May 28, 2013, section 3.1.7, http://www.ala.org/rusa/resources/guidelines/guidelinesbehavioral.

27. Reference and User Services Association, "Guidelines for Behavioral Performance," section 3.1.8.

28. Reference and User Services Association, "Guidelines for Behavioral Performance," section 5.1.1.

29. "Guidelines for Formatting Electronic Texts," January 17, 2011, http://www.uta.fi/FAST/PK5/e-format.html.

30. Reference and User Services Association, "Guidelines for Behavioral Performance," section 2.2.3.

31. Shiyali Ramamrita Ranganathan, *The Five Laws of Library Science* (New York: Asia, 1963), 9.

32. Reference and User Services Association, "Guidelines for Behavioral Performance," sections 1.3.2 and 2.3.1.

# Bibliography

Abbott, John P., and Allan G. Scherlen. "National Union Catalog: Asset or Albatross?" *Proceedings of the Charleston Library Conference* (2013): 91. http://docs.lib.purdue.edu/charleston/2012/Collection/1/.

Abels, Eileen G. "The E-Mail Reference Interview." *RQ* 35, no. 3 (1996): 345–58.

Association of College and Research Libraries. "Information Literacy Competency Standards for Higher Education." January 18, 2000. http://www.ala.org/acrl/standards/informationliteracycompetency.

Baxa, Philip C., and M. William Krasilovsky. "*Dawson v. Hinshaw Music, Inc.*: The Fourth Circuit Revisits Arnstein and the Intended Audience Test." *Fordham Intellectual Property, Media and Entertainment Law Journal* 1, no. 2 (1991): 91–115.

Bishop, Bradley Wade, and Jennifer A. Bartlett. "Where Do We Go From Here? Informing Academic Library Staffing through Reference Transaction Analysis." *College and Research Libraries.* http://crl.acrl.org/content/early/2012/05/07/crl-365.full.pdf.

Bopp, Richard E., and Linda C. Smith. *Reference and Information Services: An Introduction.* 2nd ed. Englewood, CO: Libraries Unlimited, 1995.

Bunge, Charles A. "Interpersonal Dimensions of the Reference Interview: A Historical Review of the Literature." *Drexel Library Quarterly* 20, no. 2 (1984): 4–23.

Bushallow-Wilbur, Lara, Gemma DeVinney, and Fritz Whitcomb. "Electronic Mail Reference Service: A Study." *RQ* (1996): 359–71.

Campbell, Jerry D. "Clinging to Traditional Reference Services: An Open Invitation to Libref.Com." *Reference and User Services Quarterly* 39, no. 3 (2000): 223–27. http://search.proquest.com/docview/217942772?accountid=8459.

Carlson, Scott. "Are Reference Desks Dying Out?" *Chronicle of Higher Education* 53, no. 33 (April 20, 2007): A37–A39.

Carnegie, Dale. *How to Win Friends and Influence People.* New York: Simon & Schuster, 1981.

Chow, Anthony S., and Rebecca A. Croxton. "A Usability Evaluation of Academic Virtual Reference Services." *College and Research Libraries.* http://crl.acrl.org/content/early/2013/02/06/crl13-408.full.pdf.

Conner, M. "What a Reference Librarian Should Know." *Library Journal* 52, no. 8 (1927): 415–18.

Cottrell, Janet R., and Michael B. Eisenberg. "Applying an Information Problem-Solving Model to Academic Reference Work: Findings and Implications." *College and Research Libraries* 62, no. 4 (2001): 334–47.

Damerow, Gail, ed. *Barnyard in Your Backyard: A Beginner's Guide to Raising Chickens, Ducks, Geese, Rabbits, Goats, Sheep, and Cattle.* North Adams, MA: Storey Books, 2002.

Davidson, Sarah, and Susan Mikkelsen, "Desk Bound No More: Reference Services at a New Research University Library," *Reference Librarian* 50, no. 4 (2009): 346–55.

Dawson, Patricia H. "Are Science, Engineering, and Medical Libraries Moving Away from the Reference Desk? Results of a Survey of New Jersey Libraries." *Science and Technology Libraries* 30, no. 4 (2011): 343–53.

Dennison, Russell F. "Usage-Based Staffing of the Reference Desk: A Statistical Approach." *Reference and User Services Quarterly* 39, no. 2 (1999): 158–65.

Dervin, Brenda, and Patricia Dewdney. "Neutral Questioning: A New Approach to the Reference Interview." *RQ* 25, no. 4 (1986): 506–13.

Downie, J. Stephen. "Jumping off the Disintermediation Bandwagon: Reharmonizing LIS Education for the Realities of the 21st Century." 2009. http://people.lis.illinois.edu/~jdownie/alise99/.

Dowswell, Paul, and Tony Allan. *True Ghost Stories*. Tulsa, OK: EDC, 2006.

Driver, Michaela. "Improving Group Learning through Electronically Facilitated Skillful Discussions." *Learning Organization*, 10, no. 5 (2003): 383–93.

Dubnjakovic, Ana. "Electronic Resource Expenditure and the Decline in Reference Transaction Statistics in Academic Libraries." *Journal of Academic Librarianship* 38, no. 2 (2012): 94–100.

Edwards, Jack E., Marie D. Thomas, Paul Rosenfeld, and Stephanie Booth-Kewley. *How to Conduct Organizational Surveys: A Step-by-Step Guide*. Thousand Oaks, CA: Sage, 1997.

Ewing, Keith, and Robert Hauptman. "Is Traditional Reference Service Obsolete?" *Journal of Academic Librarianship* 21, no. 1 (1995): 3–6.

Fillpot, Elise A. "A Study of Selected Variables Associated with Freshman Attrition at the University of Iowa [PhD diss., University of Iowa, 2004]." *Dissertation Abstracts International* 65:4486.

Ford, Barbara. "From Discussion to Action: Changing Reference Service Patterns." *Journal of Academic Librarianship* 18, no. 5 (1992): 285.

Fraser, Lindsey. *Conversations with J. K. Rowling*. New York: Scholastic, 2001.

Freides, Thelma. "Current Trends in Academic Libraries." *Library Trends* 31, no. 3 (1983): 457–74.

Fritch, John W., and Scott B. Mandernack. "The Emerging Reference Paradigm: A Vision of Reference Services in a Complex Information Environment." *Library Trends* 50, no. 2 (2001): 286–305.

Gladwell, Malcolm. *The Tipping Point: How Little Things Can Make a Big Difference*. New York: Little, Brown, 2002.

Green, Samuel Swett. "The Desirableness of Establishing Personal Intercourse and Relations between Librarians and Readers." *American Library Journal* 1, no. 1 (1876): 74–81.

"Guidelines for Formatting Electronic Texts." January 17, 2011. http://www.uta.fi/FAST/PK5/e-format.html.

Hammill, Sarah Jane, and Eduardo Fojo. "Using Secret Shopping to Assess Student Assistant Training." *Reference Services Review* 41, no. 3 (2013): 8–18.

Harmeyer, Dave. "Online Virtual Chat Library Reference Service: A Quantitative and Qualitative Analysis [PhD diss., Pepperdine University, 2007]." *Dissertation Abstracts International* 68/10.

———. "Virtual Reference: Less Is More." *Reference Librarian* 48, no. 1 (2007): 113–16.

Hernon, Peter, and Charles R. McClure. "Unobtrusive Reference Testing: The 55 Percent Rule." *Library Journal* 111, no. 7 (1986): 37–41.

Herriot, James. *All Creatures Great and Small*. New York: St. Martin's Press, 1972.

Hirko, Buff. "VET: The Virtual Evaluation Toolkit." 2004. http://vrstrain.spl.org/textdocs/VETmanual.pdf.

Hisle, Lee W. "Reference Questions in the Library of the Future." *Chronicle of Higher Education* 52, no. 6 (2005): B7.

Hsieh, Ma Lei, Susan McManimon, and Sharon Yang. "Faculty-Librarian Collaboration in Improving Information Literacy of Educational Opportunity Program Students." *Reference Services Review* 41, no. 2 (2013): 313–35.

Inge, M. Thomas, ed. *Conversations with William Faulkner.* Jackson: University Press of Mississippi, 1999.

Janes, Joseph. "What Is Reference For?" *Reference Services Review* 31, no. 1 (2003): 22–25.

Johnson, Corey M. "Online Chat Reference: Survey Results from Affiliates of Two Universities." *Reference and User Services Quarterly* 43, no. 3 (2004): 237–48.

Khosrowjerdi, Mahmood, and Mohammad Iranshahi. "Prior Knowledge and Information-Seeking Behavior of PhD and MA Students." *Library and Information Science Research* 33, no. 4 (2011): 331–35.

Krejcie, Robert V., and Daryle W. Morgan. "Determining Sample Size for Research Activities." *Educational and Psychological Measurements* 30 (1970): 607–10.

Kwon, Nahyun. "Assessing Virtual Reference Success Using 2004 RUSA Behavioral Guidelines." Paper presented at the Sixth Annual Virtual Reference Desk Conference, Cincinnati, OH. http://www.vrd2004.org/proceedings/.

Kwon, Nahyun, and Vicki L. Gregory. "The Effects of Librarians' Behavioral Performance on User Satisfaction in Chat Reference Services." *Reference and User Services Quarterly* 47, no. 2 (2007): 137–48.

Kyrillidou, Martha, and Les Bland, eds. *ARL Statistics 2007–2009.* Washington, DC: Association of Research Libraries, 2009 (8). http://publications.arl.org/ARL-Statistics-2008-2009.

LaGuardia, Cheryl. "The Future of Reference: Get Real!" *Reference Services Review* 31, no 1 (2003): 39–42.

Luo, Lili. "Chat Reference Competencies: Identification from a Literature Review and Librarian Interviews." *Reference Services Review* 35. no. 2 (2007): 195–209.

Lynch, Mary Jo. "Reference Interviews in Public Libraries." *Library Quarterly* 48, no. 2 (1978): 119–42.

Mathews, Brian. "While Reference Stats Decline, Oregon Surges +51%: A Glimpse at Some ARL Outliers." *The Ubiquitous Librarian* (blog). http://theubiquitouslibrarian.typepad.com/the_ubiquitous_librarian/2008/12/while-reference-stats-decline-oregon-surges-51-a-glimpse-at-some-arl-outliers.html.

McDaniel, Julie Ann, and Judith K. Ohles. *Training Paraprofessionals for Reference Service: A How-to-Do-It Manual for Librarians.* New York: Neal-Schuman, 1993.

Miller, Jerome K., and William Aguilar. "Public Library Use by Members of the Old Order Amish Faith." *RQ* 23, no. 3 (1984): 322–26.

Miller, William. "What's Wrong with Reference? Coping with Success and Failure at the Reference Desk." *American Libraries* 15, no. 5 (1984): 303–6, 321–22.

Moyer-Gusé, Emily, and Robin L. Nabi. "Explaining the Effects of Narrative in an Entertainment Television Program: Overcoming Resistance to Persuasion." *Human Communication Research* 36, no. 1 (2010): 26–52.

Norvig, Peter. "Search in '2020 Visions.'" *Nature* 463 (2010): 26.

Nozomi, Ikeya. "Approaches in the Studies of Reference Process and Its Integration: Focusing on the Studies of Reference Interviews." *Library and Information Science* 30 (1992): 43–58.

"Nurses Are in Demand." *NursingLink* (2007). http://edu.nursinglink.com/.

O'Gorman, Jack, and Barry Trott. "What Will Become of Reference in Academic and Public Libraries?" *Journal of Library Administration* 49. no. 33 (2007): 329.

Online Computer Library Center. "2,000,000,000 Holdings and Growing . . . " http://www.oclc.org/en-US/worldcat.html.

"The Online Writing Lab (OWL) at Purdue University." http://owl.english.purdue.edu/owl/.

Pomerantz, Jeffrey, Scott Nicholson, Yvonne Belanger, and R. David Lankes. "The Current State of Digital Reference: Validation of a General Digital Reference Model through a Survey of Digital Reference Services." *Information Processing and Management* 40 no. 2 (2004): 347–63.

"ProQuest's Teacher Mini-debate Guide." October 2007. http://www.proquestk12.com/productinfo/pdfs/MiniDebate_Teachers.pdf.

Radcliff, Carolyn J. "Interpersonal Communication with Library Patrons: Physician-Patient Research Models." *RQ* 24, no. 4 (1995): 497–506.

Radford, Marie. "In Synch? Evaluating Chat Reference Transcripts." In Fifth Annual Digital Reference Conference, San Antonio, TX, November 17–18, 2003. http://www.vrd2003.org/proceedings/presentation.cfm?PID=231.

Radford, Marie L., and Scott Vine. "An Exploration of the Hybrid Reference Service Model: Keeping What Works." In *Reference Reborn: Breathing New Life into Public Services Librarianship*, edited by Diane Zabel, 79–91. Santa Barbara, CA: Libraries Unlimited/ABC Clio, 2011.

Ranganathan, Shiyali Ramamrita. *The Five Laws of Library Science*. New York: Asia, 1963.

Reed, Pamela G. "Developmental Resources and Depression in the Elderly: A Longitudinal Study." *Nursing* 35, no. 6 (1986): 368–74.

Reference and User Services Association. "Guidelines for Behavioral Performance of Reference and Information Services." May 28, 2013. http://www.ala.org/rusa/resources/guidelines/guidelinesbehavioral.

Richardson, John V. "The Current State of Research on Reference Transactions." *Advances in Librarianship* 26 (2002): 175–230.

———. "Understanding the Reference Transaction: A Systems Analysis Perspective." *College and Research Libraries* 60, no. 3 (1999): 211–22.

Richardson, John V., and Rex B. Reyes. "Government Information Expert Systems: A Quantitative Evaluation." *College and Research Libraries* 56, no. 3 (1995): 235–47.

Robinson, Catherine M., and Peter Reid. "Do Academic Enquiry Services Scare Students?" *Reference Services Review* 35, no. 3 (2007): 405–24.

Ross-Gordon, Jovita M. "Research on Adult Learners: Supporting the Needs of a Student Population That Is No Longer Nontraditional." *Peer Review* 13, no. 1 (2011): 26–29.

Ryan, Susan M. "Reference Transactions Analysis: The Cost-Effectiveness of Staffing a Traditional Academic Reference Desk." *Journal of Academic Librarianship* 34, no. 5 (2008): 389–99.

Saxton, Matthew L. "Reference Service Evaluation and Meta-analysis: Findings and Methodology Issues." *Library Quarterly* 67, no. 3 (1997): 267–89.

Saxton, Matthew L., and John V. Richardson. *Understanding Reference Transactions: Transforming an Art into a Science*. San Diego, CA: Academic Press, 2002.

Schulte, Stephanie J. "Eliminating Traditional Reference Services in an Academic Health Sciences Library: A Case Study." *Journal of the Medical Library Association* 99, no. 4 (2011): 273–79.

Sears, Minnie Earl. *Sears List of Subject Headings*. Edited by Joseph Miller. New York: Wilson, 2007.

Skinner, Deborah, and Lisa Bunker. "Accio Quote! The Largest Archive of J. K. Rowling Interviews on the Web." http://www.accio-quote.org/index.html.

Sloan, B. "Asking Questions in the Digital Library: Can Users Define a VR Service?" Paper presented at the Fifth Annual Digital Reference Conference, Chicago, 2002. http://www.vrd.org/conferences/vrd2002/ proceedings/sloan.shtml.

Smith, Kenneth Harold. "The Effectiveness of Computer-Assisted Instruction on the Development of Rhythm Reading Skills among Middle School Instrumental Students [Phd diss., University of Illinois at Urbana-Champaign, 2002]." *Dissertation Abstracts International* 63:3891.

Smyth, Joanne. "Virtual Reference Transcript Analysis: A Few Models." *Searcher* 11, no. 3 (2003): 26–30.

Stevens, Christy R. "Reference Reviewed and Re-envisioned: Revamping Librarian and Desk-Centric Services with LibStARs and LibAnswers." *Journal of Academic Librarianship* 39, no. 2 (2013): 202–14.

Stowell Bracke, Marianne, Michael Brewer, Robyn Huff-Eibl, Daniel R. Lee, Robert Mitchell, and Michael Ray, "Finding Information in a New Landscape: Developing New Service and Staffing Models for Mediated Information Services." *College and Research Libraries* 68, no. 3 (2007): 248–67.

Taylor, Robert S. "Question-Negotiation and Information Seeking in Libraries." *College and Research Libraries* 29, no. 3 (1968): 178–94.

Tompson, Sara, and Catherine Quinlan. "Reference Desk Renaissance: Connecting with Users in the Digital Age." *ACRL* (March 30–April 2, 2011): 369, 371, 372. http://0-www.ala.org.catalog.wblib.org/acrl/sites/ala.org.acrl/files/content/conferences/confsandpre-confs/national/2011/papers/reference_desk.pdf.

"Updated Pricing for Educational and Nonprofit Institutions." *Linden Lab.* July 24, 2013. http://community.secondlife.com/t5/Featured-News/Updated-Pricing-for-Educational-and-Non-profit-Institutions/ba-p/2098039.

VanderVeer, Lisa. "The Function of Spirituality, Social Interest, Life Satisfaction, and Materialism in Moderating Death Anxiety in College Students [PhD diss., Adler School of Professional Psychology, 2009]." *Dissertation Abstracts International* 73/07E.

Wang, Peiling, and Dagobert Soergel. "A Cognitive Model of Document Use during a Research Project: Study I. Document Selection." *Journal of the American Society for Information Science* 49, no. 2 (1998): 115–33.

Wasik, Joann M. "Digital Reference Evaluation." June 30, 2003. http://www.vrd.org/AskA/digref_assess.shtml.

Watzlawick, Paul, Janet Beavin Bavelas, Don D. Jackson, and Bill O'Hanlon. *Pragmatics of Human Communication: A Study of Interactional Patterns, Pathologies, and Paradoxes.* New York: Norton, 1967.

Weir, Margaret. "Of Magic and Single Motherhood [interview with J. K. Rowling]." *Salon* 31 (March 1999).

Whitson, William L. "Differentiated Service: A New Reference Model." *Journal of Academic Librarianship* 21, no. 2 (1995): 103–10.

Wilson, David L. "An Exploratory Study on the Players of Dungeons and Dragons [PhD diss., Institute of Transpersonal Psychology, 2007]." *Dissertation Abstracts International* 68/07.

Wu, Mei-Mei, and Ying-Hsang Liu. "Intermediary's Information Seeking, Inquiring Minds, and Elicitation Styles." *Journal of the American Society for Information Science and Technology* 54, no. 12 (2003): 1117–33.

# Index

# About the Author

**Dave Harmeyer** is professor and associate dean of university libraries at California's Azusa Pacific University (APU). Dave is passionate about the reference interview and suggests it's one of the sustaining merits of the library and information science profession. In 2007, he completed a doctorate in educational technology from Pepperdine University, writing a dissertation on an empirical study of chat reference interviews. Dave is a column editor for *The Reference Librarian* where he writes narratives about the reference interview. To keep up with the practice, he continues to hold weekly reference desk hours and monitors a 24/7 chat reference service. Dave lives with his wife Sheli and two daughters, Breanna and Sophia, in southern California.

CPSIA information can be obtained at www.ICGtesting.com
Printed in the USA
BVOW07s0002290114

343282BV00001B/3/P